*An
Exodus
for the
Church*

An Exodus for the Church

William F. Keucher

Judson Press, Valley Forge

AN EXODUS FOR THE CHURCH

Library of Congress Cataloging in Publication Data

Keucher, William F
    An exodus for the church.

    Includes bibliographical references.
    1. Christianity—20th century. I. Title.
[BR121.2.K47]   260   72-7591
ISBN 0-8170-0508-0

To the glory of God
and in
gratitude
to
the staff, pastors, and people
of
the Kansas Baptist Convention

Foreword

"Where sin increased, God's grace increased much more" (Romans 5:20 TEV). God's people always are engaged in an exodus. God's sovereign grace always precedes and stands over his people as a cloud by day and a pillar of fire by night.

My friend William F. Keucher is among that select company of God's redeemed servants who is gifted with a disciplined life. penetrating mind, and facile pen dedicated to the church of Jesus Christ. I have often remarked to my wife, Elizabeth, that the fruitage of Dr. Keucher's wide and deep reading, power of organized thought, ability to recall, sense of the appropriate, and awareness of the Christian world should be expressed in writing. This volume is a fulfillment not only of my hopes but also the hopes of many.

We have noted with more than passing interest the pilgrimage of several who out of concern for the renewal of the visible and organized body of Jesus Christ have resigned from other forms of kingdom service and have become the pastor of a local congregation. The number may be few compared with the exodus of ordained men and seminarians who are traveling in the opposite direction. But as they join with the prophets of the living God who have continued as pastors, that cloud, the size of a man's hand, that is on the horizon is being seeded. Some contemporary and unexpected seeders who have been making me uncomfortable are Carl F. H. Henry, Sherwood Wirt, Leighton Ford, David O. Mobert, and now Bill Keucher. Who is being used of the Holy Spirit to speak to you? I trust that this volume, *An Exodus for the Church,* will be the means of seeding your cloud of divine discontent.

The modern renewal of the church is in its first stages. Diagnosis is a necessity. We are stalled by our inward and outward bondage. We are largely without the presence and power of the living Christ. We are captive to our unexamined assumptions, unreformed creeds, institutions, intractability, cultural and social conventions, modern Levites, and disengagement. We are also powerless as we have fatted our hearers on the starch of topical preaching instead of the high protein of exposition. Many of us today panic at the thought of a charismatic ministry and throw the switch. Others are simply locked in by fear of substantive change.

How many of us have moved out of Ur? God has spoken to all of us, and some have moved as far as Haran. The traffic is rush-hour heavy at this crossroads, however. Though we do not want to check in at Terah's Motel, yet the Abraham Memorial Highway is not an eight-lane interstate. It is narrow and traveled only by a few audacious souls. But these are the ones who by faith move toward the final purposes of God. They are led by the ever-living Christ who is surety for a never dying church which, washed in his blood, will be presented to the Father "without spot or wrinkle or any such thing."

J. LESTER HARNISH

Contents

1
An Exodus
from the Church

A recent Associated Press dispatch, dateline Pittsburg, Kansas, reported the following incident:

Mount Carmel Hospital here has a small building which contains a gasoline-driven generator which can be started up quickly should electrical power fail for a time at the four-story medical facility.

Recently, power failed and all electrical units in the hospital halted, including the elevators. In one of the elevators, which was stopped between floors, a trapped man began pounding on the doors of the cage and shouting for help.

A nurse, thinking to calm down the caged man, said, "Don't be alarmed, the maintenance man will soon get the auxiliary unit started and we will have power again."

But inside the cage came a shout: "I am the maintenance man!"

The ludicrous predicament of this hapless fellow, trapped inside his stalled elevator, illustrates the plight of many persons related to the official life of the church in America. Pastors and church moderators, stated clerks and board chairmen, denominational executives and church members alike—all of whom are expected to help restore power and to give leadership to the church when it is stalled—appear to be stalled and trapped themselves inside the official machinery in the life of the church. As a result, the contemporary church in its traditional forms in American life seems to be in trouble. In the words of Hezekiah recorded when, as king, he and his nation faced enslavement at the hands of the Assyrian army: "This day is a day of trouble . . . because the children are come to the time of birth and there is no strength to bring them forth" (2 Kings 19:3, author's paraphrase).

We have experienced a strange contradiction in that, while the traditional church has been suffering from a sense of impotence and frustrating failure with little apparent progress, the rock opera *Jesus Christ, Superstar* has scored a box-office smash on Broadway. During the same period, when the major "mainline" denominations have been faced with sharp budget lags and have suffered a sag in membership and attendance, the Jesus Revolution has appeared on many fronts and has received special notice by the news media with cover pictures and feature articles. Some have written and spoken helpfully about "ferment in the ministry"; others have described "a gathering storm in the churches." More seriously, we have been watching an exodus *from* the church.

An analysis of church membership figures based upon the 1971 *Yearbook of American Churches,* published by the National Council of Churches and Church Bodies, reveals that American church membership figures for the last reported year represented the lowest percentage of increase registered in modern times. Church attendance also slipped from 43 percent to 40 percent, as recorded by a Gallup Poll and reported in the *Yearbook.* This compares with previous highs in attendance at 49 percent in the years 1955 and 1958 during the decade of national religious revival. Based upon further Gallup Poll statistics, the proportion of

American adults who believe that religion is losing its influence in American life has jumped from 14 percent to 67 percent in a little more than a single decade! According to Mr. Gallup, this represents "one of the most dramatic reversals in opinion in the history of polling." [1] Coupled with the growing pessimism about the impact of religion in American life, 78 percent of those polled stated that, in their opinion, life is getting worse in terms of morals and 61 percent saw a decline of general honesty.

Louis Cassels, in a United Press International article published in 1970, indicates that a decline in giving "is causing serious financial difficulties for some American churches." One major denomination with budget askings of almost $15 million received commitments of less than $11,500,000. More than half of its eighty-nine regional groups were either unable or unwilling to meet the suggested quotas for their national budgets. National budget cuts and lags have been experienced also by Methodists, Presbyterians, and Baptists. Although the Roman Catholic church does not publish financial reports on a national basis, several of its major dioceses have been reported as operating in the red in recent years. To explain this lag and sag, Mr. Cassels identifies a range of reasons from "distrust of national church leadership, to disagreement over the nature of Christian mission, to confusion over theology, to the financial pressures of inflation on family budgets, to 'battle fatigue' among church members." [2] Another factor may be reflected in the increased competition for the donor's dollar. Recent studies indicate that churches received about 75 percent of all the money given to philanthropic causes in the United States in 1940. Eighteen years later, the church's share had declined to 51 percent with the rest going to Community Chest, hospitals, schools, and other civic causes. The last year of record, the church's share had declined to a new low of 46.8 percent.

This decline in church giving reflects what a national news weekly magazine reports as "controversy among church goers" and "a developing time of troubles in the life of American churches." In similar fashion, a women's magazine conducted a poll among one thousand of their readers, who reported widespread dissatisfaction with their church relationships.

The chief complaint was registered in the title of the article "You Can't Find God in Church Anymore." The conclusions drawn from this sampling of representative American women reveal the deep-seated feelings of doubt and alienation which lie underneath the surface because of conflicting ideas about the nature and mission of the church. Women, like men, have questions about inherited beliefs and traditional symbols. They, too, are perplexed and puzzled by tensions which emerge from conflicting views of the church as a sheltered sanctuary and rest camp, or as an unprotected sentinel post "at the front." Failing to find satisfactory answers for their questions, men and women may withhold funds, suspend their personal involvement in church activities, and, in some cases, let their membership lapse. In short, there is an exodus from the church. In addition, many, who have not yet left bodily, appear to be acting like the British mourners among the aristocracy at Lord Byron's funeral. It is said that the funeral procession contained many carriages sent by the nobility, but they were *empty*. The nobility felt that they owed some measure of perfunctory respect for a fellow peer, but they did not want their personal presence to be regarded as approval of his politics or his private life.

A recent article dealing with "The Perils of Polarization" challenges those who applaud "confrontation" as a way of shocking the church out of its indolence, even at the expense of church divisions and schism. There are some who speak approvingly of the polarization between ministers and laymen, and between denominational executives and pastors, even though the polarization leads to disaffection, dissatisfaction, and disaffiliation. Strangely enough, it appears that some of these same sources which now applaud and approve of ecclesiastical polarization were scandalized earlier by political polarization between the East and the West.[3] If our international bi-polar world, characterized by inflexible political creeds which allow no compromise of give and take, was regarded as evil, what has happened to make a sharply polarized denominational life man's highest good? If we let history teach us, we can be reminded that when men mistakenly assume that they have the final answers which allow no "give-and-take," interpersonal relationships, in politics, in business, or in the church, break down. Men then hide behind their "absolutes" except to shout at or to deride or to demolish the enemy.

Laymen and ministers, and all who have been engaged in and perhaps exhilarated by the controversial debate as to whether evangelism is personal or social, or whether the mission of the church is directed to spiritual or secular ends, have been tempted to short-circuit their discussion and to make an abrupt exodus from the church. Perhaps, instead, we need to take another look at the intensity of the existing incongruities and polarization so that we may see in them, as does James Dittes, our hope for the future.

In his book *The Church in the Way,* Dittes proposes that the task for Christian leadership is to welcome, husband, and recycle the psychic energies now being dissipated in resistance. He states: "If a member is 'fighting' what the minister wants, he also may well be fighting what he himself wants . . . he may actually be wanting what he seems to be fighting." [4] These insightful words illustrate the need for us to develop perceptions and skills which can enable us to negotiate our differences, while serving as a "guarantor" of our brother's identity and integrity. We need a style of leadership in the life of the church akin to that which Harry Levinson sees functioning in the life of the business world. This "process of reciprocation" serves to overcome the problems of distance, mobility, and change which beset every human organization. Unless these differences are "managed," people tend to use their power destructively either upon themselves or upon others in the institution. The human power available to be directed to the essential organizational tasks can never be more than that which is left over from the energy which is being used negatively rather than constructively.

In every organization, whether it is a university or a business, a club or a church, there are "psychological contracts" formed between the organization and its members. These unwritten contracts may differ from the more obviously stated organizational purposes, but they form a set of expectations which can be either fulfilled or frustrated. When they are disappointed, the power resident in us, as persons, tends to be used in some combination of four ways: "(1) directed to the task; (2) displaced from the task to some other activity; (3) contained, or not invested in either task or some other activity; and (4) directed to the self as in sickness absence, accidents, the withdrawal behavior of low morale, or injury to the organization despite its cost to the people themselves." [5]

In recent years, the contemporary church has been caught up in the whirlwind of revolutionary, worldwide change. Events have moved so rapidly that time has seldom been granted for church leaders to gain a consensus upon which they could act. Indeed, when pastors or denominational executives have acted and their actions have been consistent with official positions or resolutions adopted by their church bodies, they or their constituent members seldom understood how deeply their actions had violated some of the psychological contracts or expectations in the minds of the people. For example, one denomination elected a black person as its national leader. He was exceptionally well qualified and the election process was not different from earlier years, so that he came into office in much the same way as his predecessors. This denomination had no official policy which stipulated against having a black national president. Instead, official statements and resolutions endorsed the concept of equal access to all positions of trust in the church councils. But, nonetheless, some members of that denomination had a psychological contract which they had made, perhaps unconsciously, with the national church body. Their contract specified that the president of their religious body would always be of Caucasian stock. The election of a black president made them feel that someone had added some fine print to the original contract without their consent. The violation of their unwritten expectations led them to express their frustration and disappointment by withholding funds and by other means of passive aggression directed to the injury and the malfunctioning of the denominational agencies and purposes.

This exodus from the church and its traditional forms is not limited to laymen alone. Many ordained ministers are quietly abandoning their pastoral vocation in a search for more meaning and significance in other secular pursuits and vocational endeavors. When Sargent Shriver was the executive director of the Office of Economic Opportunity, he had so many former priests and ministers working for him that he quipped that "O.E.O. should stand for Office of Ecclesiastical Outcasts." In a recent year, in one denomination, 168 ministers left the church. Only thirty of these men entered the ministry of another denomination; apparently the remaining 138 found employment in other vocational fields. In a southern state with a very large constituent membership in one denomination, their official paper reported that out of more than five hundred pastoral changes, about 20 percent, or more than one hundred pastors, had resigned their pastorates "with their plans unannounced." Another denominational study, designed to answer the question why ministers leave the pastorate, discovered a widely ranging variety of reasons, including frustration with the church, personal problems, and better job opportunities. The three categories most stressed were conflicts with the congregation, distortion of the pastor's role, and a variety of personal problems attendant to a lack of either professional competency or satisfying meaning in the way their work was structured.

Similar stress and pressures are leading to a similar exodus in the Roman Catholic church. In 1971 Pope Paul spoke some anguished comments deploring the numbers who were abandoning the priesthood. Informal estimates suggest that more than 2500 priests have left their offices in the past seven years. A diocesan paper reports that by 1970 for every new priest ordained, two and one-half priests were lost. If trends continue unabated, the traditional priesthood faces a time of trouble.

Similarly disturbing facts are found among Protestant ministers. A Gallup Poll conducted in 1971 reported that four out of every ten ministers indicated that they would like to quit the church. In a nationwide sampling conducted early in 1971, with answers from 2517 clergymen, the results, in Mr. Gallup's opinion, underscored a major problem facing organized religion in America today—the diminishing ranks of trained leadership.

Another study of ministers who had left their pastorates revealed that system pressures have played a large role in their decisions. According to a news service article,

> These ex-pastors feel betrayed by the church system which recruited them on flimsy grounds, trained them inadequately, placed them unwisely, gave them courage to preach prophetically, then proved unwilling or unable to help them when in trouble, and then let them go with scarcely an after-thought.

The exodus from the church is not limited to the American scene exclusively. Cecil Northcott, in an article in *The Christian Century*, reported on "The Passing of the Parson." The Church of England faced the proposal to reduce the number of its theological colleges from twenty-five to fourteen. This cut reflects the decline in the number of Anglican ordinations, which have fallen below five hundred in number, although seven hundred are needed to keep up with the parish needs for clergy. Noting the air of despondency and general foreboding, we are reminded that the mood is not limited to England and its established church, but appears everywhere as a worldwide phenomenon. We are experiencing a revulsion against *institutional* Christianity—a situation which appears to be both endemic and epidemic.[6]

The exodus from the church on the part of both ministers and laymen suggests that we are facing a generation which has been described as "unlinear." The situation of the contemporary church is akin to that described in the Book of Judges, where it is recorded, "And the people served the Lord all the days of Joshua, and all the days of the elders who outlived Joshua . . . and there arose another generation after them, who did not know the Lord or the work which he had done for Israel" (Judges 2:7, 10). The church not only faces a generation with a growing distance from the Christian tradition and history, but a situation in which familiar church communities have been fractured, old symbols of religion exhausted, and the communion of Christian fellowship has been replaced by conflict, confusion, and hostility. As a result, Harry Levinson is not far off base when he is reported as saying that the ministry is probably the most besieged professional group in America. Articles dealing with the stress and effect of congregational sanctions point out that the parish minister's success is in the hands of congregational members. In other sociological studies, it is noted that the minister is expected to soft-pedal any of his views which go against the grain of public values. To different degrees for different ministers, the congregations and community succeed in socializing the minister to local values. The late Sam Miller, while serving as dean of Harvard Divinity School, said it more bluntly when he concluded that, from his observation, it took only about eighteen months for a congregation to "corrupt a minister." If churches continue to expect their professional ministry to act like "kept men," the exodus from the church can be expected to continue.

John Simpson has made a study of the Presbyterian *Confession of 1967* in an effort to understand the problem of clergy-lay conflict. He notes that any specific group which faces ambiguity in its description or definition of its role will attempt to reduce the strain and stress by *(a)* developing *new skills* or *(b)* making their new emerging role a legitimate one in organizational structures. Simpson identifies the Presbyterian *Confession of 1967* as one way in which ministers have sought to redefine and to legitimize their new understandings of what it means to be a minister of Jesus Christ in the life of the church today. Where consensus did not prevail, misunderstandings and conflicts broke out.[7] Simpson's study and its insights hold illustrative value for all our denominational structures. Significant and measurable changes are taking place in the attitudes of our ministers. They are seeing and defining their ministry in new perspectives which they feel reflect a deeper loyalty to Christ and greater faithfulness to the gospel. Unfortunately, many people in the pew neither understand nor appreciate these new roles, and they feel that their traditional expectations have been violated. Members who join the church expecting the ministry of the church to afford comfort and shelter are disturbed and alarmed when they hear the call to battle and face the demands for a costly commitment in some form of Christian social action. Pulpit committees are led to accuse seminaries of producing misfits for the pastorate. Seminaries may feel that, given the church as it is, they can be faithful to God only by producing misfits for churches as they are.

The exodus from the churches, with declining attendance, sagging financial support, and leadership defections, reflects the serious level of frustration and disappointment which has been experienced in our major denominational bodies. Pastors, as all studies have shown rather conclusively, experience stress because they see the mission of the church and their professional role in it quite differently from the way many church members see things. Church members themselves suffer stress because if they thought of themselves as having volunteered for the Lord's army at all, they expected duty in the quartermaster corps. Their secret contractual arrangements were violated when they were asked to march to Selma or to be a part of a picket parade in Washington, D.C., or at city hall in their own community. The church which they had joined, as they saw it, was not designed to be an expeditionary force meant to interfere in the life of the secular world by direct political action or by economic boycotts or by social sanctions. What did all these have to do with the main business of the church which they believed the New Testament set forth so clearly, to "preach the gospel" and "to win souls to Christ"?

Our situation is complicated by the very way in which the church is organized and sees itself functioning as a Christian fellowship. Other areas of society are organized on a clear adversary basis. In law, there is a plaintiff and a defendant. Cases are heard and judges and juries decide in favor of either the plaintiff or the defendant. In business, the demands between capital and labor must be negotiated and often arbitrated. In business, bids are sought, and one is accepted on the basis of its most favorable terms and the ability of the bidder to perform in satisfying the contractual expectations. In politics, candidates within the same party vie with each other for their party's nomination. Subsequently, in most elections, there are at least two candidates for each office. But how is it in the life of the church? We affirm verbally that there is room for pluralism, but few churches are organized to allow measurable dissonance or dissent to appear. In actual experience "conflict" is associated with unchristian attitudes. Church members are supposed to be "nice" people. Church fellowship must never be disturbed by controversial issues. As a result, the only avenue open to many church members who want to join issues is to "sound off" in a church meeting and be branded as inferior Christians, or to withdraw in some form of passive aggression designed to sabotage the church organization.

It may be apparent, by this time, that I am not writing as a dispassionate observer of American church life. My experience as a denominational executive for eighteen years does not allow me to be either academic or objective. These good years, filled with so much personal meaning, represent a heavy psychological investment in the institutional life of the church. Thus, a reflective reader may have already suspected why my eyes were attracted to the maintenance man trapped in his stalled elevator and why I was led to report this incident in the beginning of this book. You are right. As a church executive, I saw myself in the illustration! And I saw most of my colleagues suffering the same kind of "Egyptian" bondage. In the eighteen years of close association with pastors and laymen, I came to understand the nature of their frustrations and disappointments which distressed their souls and brought them into similar circumstances of servitude. The stalled elevator turned out to be a very crowded place, filled with "maintenance men" from all levels and sectors of our contemporary church life.

More recently, I was led into a personal exodus of my own, from the executive and so-called administrative life of the church, to serve once again as pastor of a single congregation. In taking that step, I explained my action in part by saying "the lenses we wear are ground to the prescription of our textbooks and our teachers. . . . A certain image is fitted to our eyes. We grow accustomed to the image. But every so often comes a time for optical reexamination." Knowing that the pastorate was a beleaguered profession, I felt that I must sit where the pastors sat if I was to be able to understand their feelings and their situations and to break out of the distressing stereotypes which the expectations of other people build into relationships of long standing. Knowing also that the local congregation was under fire (often from myself!) as an archaic impediment to the needed progress in God's kingdom, I felt convicted by the growing awareness that our world needs critical lovers more than unloving critics. Knowing also the reasons for polarization between denominational executives and constituent churches, as well as between pastors and laymen, and between laymen themselves, I wanted to use whatever insight and experience I had to seed the clouds gathering in storm over the life of the churches.

What has been the result of my personal exodus from official executive leadership to pastoral leadership? I must confess that only the stage and setting have been changed. The script and the characters remain essentially the same! Whether one is serving his denomination as an elected executive, or whether one is serving as a pastor or as a lay member, he discovers that the church is stalled in many of its efforts to fulfill its mission, and many members share the frustrating feeling that they, themselves, are trapped inside the life of the church in a kind of Egyptian bondage.

A recent Charlie Brown comic strip contains as much "bad news" as "good news." Lucy is in her booth ready to give psychiatric aid. Charlie Brown muses as much to himself as to Lucy, as he looks up into the sky: "See that plane up there? It's filled with people who are all going someplace. That's what I'd like to do, go off somewhere someplace and start a new life." Lucy responds, "Forget it, Charlie Brown,—when you got off the plane, you'd still be the same person you are." Charlie Brown objects, "But maybe when I got to this new place, the new people would like me better." Lucy chills his hopes, "Only until they got to know you, Charlie Brown; then you'd be right back where you started." But Charlie persists, "But maybe these new people would be more understanding." Lucy ends the consultation on a note of final certainty, "People are people, Charlie Brown."

Lucy's word seems to be such a final one: People are people! We are locked into our personal histories as well as into our genetic origins. We are locked into our social situations and the pressure of our existing environment. "People are people"; that judgment seems implicit in the fated determinism which concludes, "You can't change either human nature or social situations."

Though I may function at times with that hopelessness, I refuse to accept the legitimacy of that pessimistic determinism either about men or about the church. The good news of the Christian faith and gospel declares that men do not need to stay the way they are. Trapped by their past and in present circumstances, the grace of God is able to reach them and to provide a way out in Jesus Christ. The faith and vision of people can be released as a constructive force in the life of the church to bring about change and renewal. There is a way out of personal or institutional bondage and captivity. Denominational executives, church pastors, and lay people, together, can learn a new style of mutual commitment, consistent with the integrity of the gospel and with a compassionate, confirming concern about what is happening to people inside as well as outside the church. To avert a continuing exodus from the church, we need a new exodus *for* the church which can free the people of God for their Christian mission, evangelistic witness, Christlike service, and faithful action.

2
A New Exodus from Egypt to Emmaus

The church in America is in trouble. Dissipating its energies destructively, declining in influence and impact, the church is facing disloyalty among its members and defection among its leaders. Impotent where it should be strong, divided where it should be united, cautious and prudent where it should be courageous and prophetic, silent when it should be vocal, immobilized by conflicts within, the church may be seen in various sectors of her life, helpless and hapless in the face of urban mobility and change which characterize our society.

We have affirmed that only an exodus *for* the church can avert a continuing exodus *from* the church. Few emigrants know what their new life will be like; what they know best is why they are leaving. Just as it seems more difficult for a man to tell you what he is *for* rather than what he is against, so to call for an exodus for the church poses the problem of doing more than identifying the nature of the captivity in which the church languishes in servile bondage. We must also see that an exodus includes "a way out *from*," and also "a way *into.*" An exodus from Egypt and its bondage will include deliverance from the conditions which cripple, impede, and thwart the life of the church from being faithful to its mission and to the trust it has received in the Christian gospel. Life in Egypt for the people of Israel, as slaves, meant a life of bondage and servitude. As slaves, they knew deprivation and loss. Their bondage meant a loss of freedom to move from place to place and to act with flexible mobility. Their bondage meant a loss of self-determination with the concomitant loss of freedom to choose meaningful options. As slaves, they were free to do only what the conditions of their bondage permitted. Their bondage meant a loss of personhood and identity with a consequent loss of meaning and significance. Without a voice or a vote in their daily life, they lived, at best, a marginal life amid the cultural. political, and social affairs of Egypt. When, finally, they were delivered by God out of their Egyptian bondage, we discover that, as former slaves, they did not know what to do with their freedom!

The Old Testament records the story of the first Exodus (cf. Exodus 12), celebrating God's saving actions which led Israel out of their Egyptian captivity and set them free to be his people. Israel, no matter how far the nation lapsed in its faith and faithfulness, could never forget the founding event of their exodus deliverance which took them as "no people" and made them "God's people" (cf. Hosea 2:21-23), bearing his name together with the responsibility of witnessing to all the nations of the earth to the light of his truth and his everlasting mercy.

We believe that a new exodus for the church is possible because in the New Testament we see the fulfillment of God's saving actions in Jesus Christ which led him to send "his only begotten Son" into the midst of the world in the fullness of times, to deliver men from their lifelong bondage to sin and the fear of death. It is significant that when Jesus announces his mission in Nazareth (Luke 4:18-19), he is led to quote the prophet Isaiah:

"The Spirit of the Lord is upon me,
because he has anointed me to preach good news to the poor.
He has sent me to proclaim release to the captives
and recovering of sight to the blind,
to set at liberty those who are oppressed,
to proclaim the acceptable year of the Lord."

The claim of Jesus is quite clear. The King brings the kingdom of God with him, together with God's year of jubilee (the acceptable year). God's act of redemption and reconciliation in Jesus Christ has provided the basis for a new start for humanity. In the year of jubilee, slaves were set free, debts were canceled, leases expired, and the land was restored to its original owners (cf. Leviticus 25). The jubilee gave the people of Israel a brand new start. So, Christ affirms that his coming into the life of the world means a new beginning for its life and history. Familiar words of the New Testament have become so commonplace in our hearing that they have lost something of the authentic and of the revolutionary and cosmic scope of God's action which makes the gospel good news rather than bad news for the world. "God so loved the world that he gave his only Son, that whoever believes in him should not perish but have eternal life" (John 3:16). "God was in Christ reconciling the world to himself . . . and entrusting to us the message ot reconciliation" (2 Corinthians 5:19). "[Jesus] is the propitiation for our sins: and not for ours only, but also for the sins of the whole world" (1 John 2:2, KJV). They shall come from the east and from the west and from the north and from the south and sit together in the kingdom of God (cf. Matthew 8:11). Christ has deposed the powers of sin and darkness and has cast down the prince of the present age and has released the powers of a new age for man's appropriation. All these sayings are a part of a total testimony which affirms that God's action in Jesus Christ has personal consequences for the man who believes, and a cosmic meaning and significance as well.

The early church affirmed they did not see all things yet subject to Christ, but they did have a vision of Christ (cf. Hebrews 2:8-9). They believed that God had acted to give men a glimpse into the way history will be completed within the providence of God's purpose. Like a man engrossed in a mystery story, who is allowed to see the end of the story before he has finished reading it, the world is afforded a confidence through Jesus Christ which assures us that "this is the victory that overcomes the world, our faith" (1 John 5:4). Jesus is God's last word to man, because history is in the process of becoming "His story" and all events are moving together to find their ultimate meaning and significance in Christ's life and work.

The Good News of the gospel must be described as both objective and subjective. The church does not make its own gospel, but it receives the gospel as a gift of God based on the events of Christ's birth, life, death, resurrection, and ascension. His total life story stands as a series of events in history which cannot be changed or altered by the popular action of the church. If sixty-six persons out of one hundred voted that Christ did not suffer the just for the unjust to bring men to God, their vote would represent a majority opinion, but it would not change the nature of the event itself. In this sense, God's action in Christ to provide the world with an exodus from death to life, from sin to salvation, from servitude to sonship, stands on its own merit as a work of divine grace. The gospel has a meaning, validity, and worldwide scope, whatever individual men may say or think or do about it.

Bishop Nygren illustrates this fact by relating an incident from the Second World War. The Norwegian countries had been invaded and were being occupied by alien powers. After several years of fearful life under the yoke of their bondage and occupation, one day a message swept across the Scandinavian countries, "Denmark is free! Norway is free!" What had happened? A power stronger than the occupying powers had come and had deposed them and deprived them of their unlawful dominion. Bishop Nygren observes, "That is the objective thing which has taken place. But—and this is the other no less important side of the matter—at the same time a stupendous transformation of each individual's subjective situation has taken place." [1] We must understand

clearly that God's redemption in Jesus Christ, in terms of its reconciling action, has a worldwide social significance while, at the
same time, it encounters each man personally and says "whoever
will" may freely come. The good news of the gospel is that God has
acted decisively so that we can be delivered from our Egyptian
bondage; the bad news related to it is that we can reject God's grace
and frustrate his purpose for ourselves. God has given to us the
responsibility to make our decision.

Our personal and our ecclesiastical bondage in Egypt is very
real. Bondage in Egypt for the contemporary church includes captivity to our unconscious assumptions, captivity to our
unreformed religious creeds, captivity to our unyielding and inflexible structures and stereotypes, captivity to uncritical, cultural,
and social conventions and majorities, and captivity to a marginal
style of life within the church which encourages our historical
disengagement and absenteeism. In subsequent chapters we shall
be dealing with this bondage under the themes, "Exodus from
Athens," "Exodus from Nicea," "Exodus from Jerusalem,"
"Exodus from Rome," "Exodus from Sinai," "Exodus from
Babylon to Bethlehem," and "Exodus from Haran to Antioch and
Beyond."

Our main thesis is that God's action in Jesus Christ provides
more than adequate resources to deliver us from our chains. The
same power which God used to raise Jesus Christ from the dead is
available for the life and mission of his church. T. R. Glover came
to a considered judgment which he describes in his classic entitled
The Jesus of History. His careful examination of historical sources
and records convinced him that there is a remarkable correlation
between the strongest periods of church history and the church's
grasp upon the centrality of Christ. To come into vital touch with
Jesus Christ as a Living Reality results in a measurable increase of
vitality and power for the church. To lose touch with Christ results
in a decline of contagious influence and in a more marginal
effectiveness. These warm convictions are not different from the
findings of H. R. Mackintosh who probed the extant records to
discover what is most uniquely original in the Christian message.
He sums up his discoveries in these words:

Whereas every other historic and prophetic religion makes progress by transcending its Founder, Christianity has grown in life and power in exact proportion as from time to time it recovers touch with Jesus, submits more loyally to His will, and accepts with a deeper gratitude the life of sonship He imparts.[2]

The same kind of exacting scholarship based on a lifetime of biblical studies led C. H. Dodd to a similar conclusion: "Christ in Christian faith is not merely an historical figure of the past. Theologians and simple Christians alike . . . find a mystery in His Person to which historical categories are inadequate." Thus he points out that men are led to "find in Him 'a present Saviour,' or a 'Lord and Master' to whom they are personally responsible, in a sense not applicable to any mere character in historical literature." [3]

We could say that there is a remarkable agreement that the reality of an ever living Christ is central to the assurance of a never dying church. We believe that an exodus for a church moribund in its Egyptian bondage is possible because Jesus Christ is alive forevermore. Just as two discouraged disciples discovered the risen Christ during their disconsolate walk to Emmaus, we, today, can discover that the Emmaus road has intersected every century and runs by our own church door!

We cannot overlook the danger that lies in placing too great an emphasis upon the early practitioners of a science or profession. In medicine, for example, when King Henry VIII was treated by his personal physician, one Dr. Butts, the accepted remedy for a high fever was to draw a pint or more of the patient's blood. Today, when we see our family doctor for a fever, we are glad that modern medicine has forgotten some of the early founders of medicine and their rude practices. Francis Bacon, in one of his essays, supports this understanding when he reminds us that we are wrong in thinking of the earliest periods of human existence as "ancient history," in the sense of their being old. The world of 5000 B.C. was not nearly as old as is the world of the 1970s which has added almost another seven thousand years to its history. From earlier, more primitive experience, we today are blessed with the accumulated insights, not only of the founders of science, but of their successors!

This point of view would seem to argue that Christians can afford to forget Christ. In what way does his life in the first century offer us meaning, validity, and power in the twentieth century? Jesus is spoken of as a person with final significance because, although he was born in Palestine two thousand years ago, he remains intensively inexhaustible. He is not behind us, as though the spiritual progress of the world had outdistanced him. He is ahead of us, and we confess that we are hard-pressed to keep up with him, let alone to overtake him. As a final person, he shows us the ultimate outcome of God's purposes for the world and for his people. As a final person, Jesus remains as the Way, the Truth, and the Life. Jesus is to be remembered not merely as the founder of his church, but as its present builder, who himself is the beginning and the end of all things. He is our destination as well as the Way. Every generation is equidistant to his eternal presence, quite apart from the passage of time. He stands in the midst of each generation, so that our Christian experience begins in a personal relationship to him as living Savior and grows with his abiding presence within us. In that sense, Jesus is not the founder of a religion, like Buddha or Confucius. He is "the author and the finisher of our salvation" (cf. Hebrews 12:2, KJV). Without him, the story of Christian faith cannot begin for us; and when it does begin, the story cannot be finished without the Author's continuing presence and action in us and with us.

In making this staggering claim for the Christian faith, we are not unmindful of the persistent questions which may be asked. How can a life which was lived in the first century, amid its simple, economic conditions, claim to have enduring significance for contemporary man in industrialized Western society? There seem to be large tracts of human life outside the actual life history of Jesus of Nazareth. According to the record, he was not married. How could he be touched and have understanding about the moral pressures which modern men and women experience in the age of the Pill? He never had a shift job or payments to make on a home mortgage or on the newest model automobile. How can he understand and appreciate and offer us solutions for the economic pressures of our computer age? He never ran for or held a public office. How can the politicians of the twentieth century look to Jesus for understanding of their own situation in the pressures of the political arena? He never served in the army. How could he know or understand the questions of the young man facing the problems of war and peace and conscience and the draft? He died at thirty-three, long before the time when men today are rudely pushed aside by systems of involuntary retirement. How could he understand the problems of aging, the deprivations of growing old, the boredom of leisure, the hopelessness and anonymity of urban life? He never had to live in Harlem or in any of the ghettos of our urban cities. How could he understand the feelings of the mother living in a tenement, hemmed in by the determinism of an inhuman and dehumanized social order?

To a small degree, we can attempt an answer to these questions by referring to the man whom Jesus identifies as "the Father of the faithful." When Abraham heard God's call (cf. Genesis 12:1-9), his response of faith prompted him to forsake familiar surroundings and family securities. As a pilgrim, he went out by foot or by camel train in faith. Centuries of time now separate us in the space age from the painful, tortuous trek of Abraham. The means of travel and communication between him and us are vastly different. Abraham might indeed be lost if he were to appear today in the age of the satellite. But if he could not understand some of the complexities which did not exist in his day, he still would discover a remarkable similarity between his own inward life and history and that of contemporary man. How men travel has radically altered; but why men travel has scarcely changed at all. God's call to Abraham, centuries ago, was not less existential than the divine summons, encounter, and claim is for any man today. When daily decisions involve the presence of the living God and his demand for obedience, they form a crisis theology demanding a personal response of faith, whether of Abraham, Paul, Luther, or us.

We have been claiming that the dynamic for a new exodus for the church from its Egyptian bondage lies in the reality of the new age in which the risen Christ rules as King. Men enter the new age by a new and living way through Jesus Christ (cf. Hebrews 10:19-20), who is not only the Jesus of history, but the Christ of faith.

"There is no other name under heaven given among men by which we must be saved" (Acts 4:12). He is the author of an eternal salvation (cf. Hebrews 5:9). However, the church must not be guilty of diminishing or narrowing the work of Christ by limiting it to the period of his earthly history between Bethlehem and Calvary. The period of his incarnation does represent an historic revelation of such magnitude that the writer of Hebrews is able to say, "In the past, God spoke to our ancestors many times and in many ways through the prophets, but in these last days he has spoken to us through his Son" (Hebrews 1:1-2, TEV). But he goes on to say, "through whom, God created the universe." The church may never fully appreciate the cosmic scope of the work of Christ as the full expression and agent of God's revelation. However, we must consider the meaning of his preincarnate work in the Old Testament, in Israel, and in the surrounding nations if we are to understand his continuing work, subsequent to his resurrection, accomplished by his Spirit through the church and in the world. Thus in Acts 4:12, which speaks of "no other name," we would understand this to signify that Christ's existence did not begin with his birth in Bethlehem into the world. Everywhere and always, he has been the agent of God's salvation in every period of history, even before his coming into the world in his incarnation.

It is obvious that this text in Acts does not require one to know the English name for Jesus Christ in order to know his person and nature for which all of his names would stand. Thus, Jesus said, "Abraham saw my day and rejoiced" (cf. John 8:56). The salvation which Abraham experienced by faith was no less real than the experience of the psalmist in a later day, or of the disciples when they lived in the earthly presence of the Son of man. In the Gospel of John, itself, we are reminded of its witness wherein Jesus is spoken of as the Eternal Word, "the true light that enlightens every man was coming into the world" (John 1:9). To understand the work of Christ in its widest meaning is to open a new world of impact and power in the life of the church. Subsequent to his death and resurrection, it is in our faith that he continues his work by his Spirit both in the church and in the world. The patterns of his life set forth in the first century as one "who in every respect has been tempted as we are, yet without sinning" (Hebrews 4:15), can be as final in the twentieth or in all later centuries, because He lives forever by the power of endless life (cf. Hebrews 7:24-25). In the resurrection of Christ we learn that he has been declared the "Son of God in power . . . by his resurrection from the dead" (Romans 1:4). We discover a new dynamic released in the life of the church and in our own human experience through faith, understood not merely as intellectual consent to finished propositions, but as the commitment of life to the final person in whose love and life and liberating power his church may find a way out from its bondage. "I thank God," exclaimed the apostle Paul, when he was himself trapped, "there is a way out through Jesus Christ." (Cf. Romans 7:25.) An exodus *is* a way out!

We may be helped at this point to recall our feelings when we first watched Neil Armstrong climb down the extended steps of the Lunar Module to be the first man on the moon. In a cold and hostile environment, where temperatures vary 500 degrees—243 degrees above zero in sunlight to 279 degrees below zero in shadow—man from the earth had established a foothold on the moon. Millions of people watched, with a sense of awful excitement and expectancy, as the TV camera sent back the amazing signals with the spectacular vision of the astronauts' first moonwalk. The moonwalk, itself, was made possible because of the vital support systems which the astronauts carried on their backs. As we watched, our sense of suspense increased as their supply of oxygen diminished. We began to fret, lest some unforeseen accident prevent their safe return to the Lunar Module where they could once again derive their support from the spaceship itself. Thus far, man's ability to survive in outer space is due to the fact that he brings all of the vital supplies necessary to sustain his life from the earth to the moon.

In much the same way, man's life on the earth would be as mysterious and spectacular as the astronauts' moonwalk if our walk across the earth had not become so commonplace. But, in a real sense, man's ability to sustain his life on earth is as dependent on adequate support systems as his ability to live in outer space and to walk on the surface of the moon. Man needs clean air to breath, uncontaminated food to eat, and an unpolluted environment to live in. But even more, because we are made for God, our homesickness of heart will never be really satisfied until our broken relationships with God are restored so that God's strength and love can flow into our lives on earth. The ability of a tree to send its roots deep into the earth depends on its ability to take the energy of sun and light from above. One could conclude that just as the tree must be rooted in the sky before it can live on the earth, so man's life of faith must be related to heaven before he can be effectively related to earth.

Such a telling and a victorious faith can free the church for its needed exodus. Mindful of our weakness and impotence, we hear ourselves asking the question of the disciples at the foot of the Mount of Transfiguration, as they faced a demon which had outstripped their powers, "Why could we not cast it out?" (Cf. Matthew 17:14-21.) We see ourselves with Ezekiel in his vision of a valley of dry bones, and the question leaps across the centuries to our lips, "Can these bones live?" (Cf. Ezekiel 37:3.) We find ourselves in the earliest age of man's consciousness in a place called Eden, where man's companionship with God is interrupted, where his communion and commerce with the source of his life have been broken, and the resplendent image of God reflected upon man's face has been dulled and marred. From that situation of existential despair, we, and the church of Christ itself, must walk the way to Emmaus where the risen Master can offer us a new exodus from our Egyptian bondage and captivity. We are brought once again by faith into touch with the central springs which feed the tributaries of God's people and God's world, across the centuries of time.

3
An Exodus
from Athens

A new exodus for the church leads us from Egyptian bondage by way of Emmaus where the church is equipped by the presence of Christ, through his Spirit, and given her urgent sense of mission to continue and complete his unfinished task. The church's task is made clear in the light of Christ's life and death. The range of God's love is not limited to one segment of human society. The mission of Jesus was "to seek and to save that which was lost" (cf. Luke 19:20, KJV). According to the Bible, "that" included everyone in the human family. Jesus' purpose in coming was to break down the middle wall of partition which kept men alienated from God and from each other and to gather into one the scattered branches of the human family. His cross, as we have seen, had both an objective and a subjective meaning, involving a cosmic and a social dimension, as well as a personal magnetic appeal. God had acted in Christ, not only to reconcile the world unto himself, but he had entrusted to the church the ministry and the message of reconciliation. In all of the Four Gospels, as well as in the first chapter of Acts, the Great Commission of Jesus is repeated in one form or another. The missionary and evangelistic task of God's people is clear; we are to disciple the nations. That must mean something different from making proselytes (enlisting recruits), inasmuch as Jesus commanded us to make disciples, but he condemned the making of proselytes.

For that clear task of worldwide evangelization and personal witness, the church is to receive the selfsame power which God used to raise Jesus from the dead, so that the church could be empowered with unfailing strength to witness and to work from Jerusalem throughout all Judea and Samaria to the very ends of the earth (cf. Acts 1:8). The church has been promised adequate power to accomplish its task of evangelism, Christian nurture, worldwide witness, and missionary outreach into the lives of men and nations. What has happened across the centuries to stall our progress, to frustrate our sense of mission, and to trap us in fruitless discussion and controversy about what the church is destined to be and to do in the providence of God?

One answer to this question, in part, is that the church has been taken captive by its unexamined assumptions which have emerged out of unbiblical sources and traditions. Rejecting tradition spelled with a capital "T," which would include the testimony of all the centuries including the first, we have often unconsciously received and have been shaped by the more limited traditions spelled with a little "t." As a consequence, we do not read the Bible objectively or without a personal bias. Instead, we put on the spectacles which have become so much a part of our way of seeing things that we are unaware that they are on our eyes like contact lenses. These unexamined assumptions trap us and prevent our being free or flexible enough as a church to fulfill our Christian mission to evangelize the world. Some of these unconscious assumptions emerged out of classical patterns and traditions of Greek life and culture; others emerged out of the individualism of our own American frontier. To be set free for the effective prosecution of our Christian mission, the church must have a new exodus out of Athens, away from all of these unexamined assumptions.

Herbert Butterfield reminds us that no historian can write history without his own presuppositions. He finds that the blindest of all the blind is the historian who is unable to examine his own unconscious assumptions and proceeds blithely unaware of their presence, believing that he has none. However, Butterfield asserts, "Each of us looks upon the world from a special peep-hole of his own." [1] Arthur Koestler speaks from his own seven-year association in the Communist party in which he found it possible to look at the worst years of Stalin's regime without really seeing what he saw. He discovered that he and other party members seemed to have "an automatic sorting machine in their heads." [2] During the period of the forced collectivization of the land, Koestler saw entire villages deserted, railway stations thronged by crowds of begging families with starving infants with stick-like arms, puffed-up bellies, and cadaverous heads; but his mental illusions gained from his party loyalty provided him an iron curtain against the intrusions of the harsh realities he looked at but did not see. He lived in a world which shut him in, much akin to the self-contained universe of the Middle Ages. In such a setting, a man mirrors the presuppositions and patterns of his peers and their prevailing philosophy. [3]

Thus, in much the same way, we, as Christians, read the Bible and hear the words of Jesus from the standpoint of our inherited systems of belief within the structures of the traditional religious community. Because of what we bring to the Bible, we color what it says to us quite as much as the Bible, itself, colors and shapes our views and our attitudes. Like Butterfield's historian, each Christian, each congregation, and each denomination looks upon the world of the Bible "from a special peep-hole of his own." Perhaps we can illumine this point by an illustration from a field outside the province of the church. Dr. Karl Menninger, in his book *The Vital Balance*, tells us that on January 1, 1950, in two wards at

Topeka State Hospital, there were eighty-eight patients. Their average age was sixty-eight. Fifty-one of them had been bedfast for an average of ten years. About twenty of them had no control of their bodily functions. Forty-one of them had to be spoon-fed at every meal! Dr. Menninger asks us to "picture this ward full of long-time bedridden, incontinent, hopeless, vegetating patients." Then picture a new therapeutic team of doctors, nurses, aides, social workers, and psychiatric residents who made each patient the focus of personal attention. New lights were installed, rooms were redecorated, music and handcraft work were initiated, relatives were urged to visit. A year later, *only nine* of those nearly ninety patients were still bedfast; only six were still incontinent; twelve of them were now back with their families; six of them were on their own; and four were self-supporting! What had happened to bring about such a dramatic change? Dr. Menninger says, "The glacier of public indifference" had melted.[4]

Practical decisions had been outlined in the governor's message to the legislature. New measures and new appropriations of a substantial nature were made to finance a new approach to the medical and mental health problems of the state. But beyond all this, an educational program conducted by The Menninger Foundation and others across a number of years had finally led people in positions of public trust to examine their long-held unconscious assumptions about mental health. Up to that moment, the unexamined, unconscious assumption said, "Mental illness is incurable." The unexamined, unconscious assumption said, "Crazy people require lifetime, custodial care." The unexamined, unconscious assumptions decreed that mentally disturbed persons were to be incarcerated behind barred windows and locked doors. The revolutionary approach to the mental health program, which Dr. Menninger reports, could not have taken place had not the members of the state legislature, with public understanding and support, modified their unconscious assumptions of how emotionally disturbed people were to be treated. Just as the community does not stigmatize the man who has had his appendix removed, labeling him for the rest of his life as "an appendectomy," so when the unconscious and unexamined assumptions about mental illness were brought into the light of reality, effective decisions and programs could be made leading to the social redemption of emotionally disturbed people.

The analogy seems quite clear. The unexamined, unconscious assumptions and presuppositions held by Christian people in the life of the church must be examined and, where necessary, changed and modified if the church is to experience a new exodus to fulfill its mission leading to personal and social redemption. What we want to affirm is that in the act of perceiving our world, we make our world. This statement appears to be simple, but it is profoundly provocative. Two men may look at the same world, but their individual perceptions color and complete the world which they see. What men see proves to be the creative difference between people. We can all see how this truth applies to our own experience. In perceiving our marriage, we make it. In a real sense, our marriages don't fail; we fail. The failure begins with our perceptions, inward, unconscious, and unmeasured. One day, however, these pictures have colored our thinking so that our decisions and our deeds are determined by our perceptions. Relationships are deepened or strained. In his psychological study, *Young Man Luther,* Erik Erickson indicates how the perceptions of Martin Luther afforded selective choice in forming his own identity. In like fashion it should be clear that our perceptions about the ministry and mission of Christ will give shape and substance to the way we see our own Christian mission in the church. As Christians, we perceive that we get our mandate, or marching orders, from Christ. What concerns him, we understand, should concern us. What he gave himself to and for must command our own energy and loyalty as well. If the church could have a clear perception about the mission of Jesus, the church could have a much clearer understanding about its own mission.

In reading the New Testament as a whole, we come to understand that salvation has to do with man's wholeness. Hence, we perceive that one important part of our Christian mandate must be described as personal evangelism. Man's life is broken by sin; God's love in Jesus Christ is needed to make him whole again. One of the best definitions and descriptions of evangelism, speaking to the important personal dimensions of the evangelistic task, came from a special commission appointed by Bishop William Temple. The report entitled "Towards the Conversion of England" states: "To evangelise is so to present Christ Jesus in the power of the Holy Spirit, that men shall come to put their trust in God through Him, to accept Him as their Saviour, and serve Him as their King in the fellowship of His Church." [5] The urgent necessity for personal evangelism was summed up aptly by the late D. T. Niles when he said, "Evangelism is one beggar telling other beggars where bread may be found." The important necessity for personal evangelism is made clear in the New Testament description of man's situation. He is "dead in his trespasses and sins." Only in Christ can he be made alive again.

But man is destined by God to be more than "a living soul." The first thing in the world that God pronounced as "not good" was man's being alone (cf. Genesis 2:18). The creative hand of God fashioned man also as a loving soul. The purpose of God's redemption is to restore his original intention in Creation, so that man, broken and alienated, might be re-created in the newness and the wholeness of life in Christ and become once again a living and a loving soul. The Christian mandate demands that we start with the personal and inward aspects of man's existence; the Christian mandate is equally insistent that man's outward, social relationships and responsibilities are to be claimed by Christ and come under his Lordship. If the church neglects the personal dimensions of its Christian mandate, it leaves man in his brokenness. But if the church neglects the social dimensions of its Christian mandate, it leaves man trapped in social disorder and alienation. The work of Christ includes both man's redemption and man's reconciliation. We do not perceive the gospel clearly, nor do we preach the gospel faithfully or fully, if we neglect either aspect of Christ's mission and God's intention. Redemption is personal; reconciliation is social. Christian evangelism can never be less than both personal and social, without diminishing the mandate we have received from Christ and his gospel.

The perception of this truth has profound consequences for the way a church perceives its task and organizes its energies to complete it. For example, we must refuse to fall into the trap of separating the work of Christ into compartments which never meet—like sacred and secular, spiritual and worldly. To think of Christ's work as "inward and personal" only is to abandon the world of social and outward relationships and responsibilities, as though that world is subject to another king. In his resurrection and ascension, Jesus is revealed as Lord and Christ, King of kings and Lord of lords. In his victory on the cross, the Scriptures make it plain that he acted to depose the false rulers of the world who had usurped his right to reign (cf. 1 Corinthians 2:6, Moffatt). Christians come to perceive that everything that God has made is good.

The comprehensive scope of the church's evangelistic task was described in *The World Mission of the Church*, by the Tambaram Conference in 1938, as follows:

> It is not enough to say that if we change the individual we will of necessity change the social order. This is a half truth, for the social order is not entirely made up of individuals now living. It is made up of inherited attitudes which have come down from generation to generation through customs, laws, institutions, and these exist in large measure independently of individuals now living. Change these individuals and you do not of necessity change the social order unless you organise these changed individuals into collective action. . . . While it is a half truth to say that changed individuals will necessarily change the social order, it is also a half truth to say that social change will necessarily produce individual change. We cannot sustain a new social order or bring it into being without new men, for in the ultimate analysis the whole outer structure of society rests upon human character.[6]

In the light of this statement, we perceive that the social order in America has an existence, a direction and a momentum which got started before we were born and which exists largely independently of those of us who happen to be alive now. We see this point quite clearly when we think about the institution of human slavery which was a part of the American social order in an earlier period of our history. The institution of slavery did not get changed merely by changing individuals. Thousands of people experienced a sincere conversion to Christ, but because they kept reading their Bibles with unexamined assumptions, nothing happened as a result of their conversion to interfere with the inhumanity of slavery. For the institution of slavery to be changed from an accepted social practice, it required President Lincoln's Emancipation Proclamation; it required laws to be passed, such as the Fourteenth Amendment to the United States Constitution; it required adjustments in our social institutions; most deeply, it required changes in our unconscious assumptions which could then be reflected in the national fabric of American life. In the Dred Scott decision, the United States Supreme Court ruled that slaves were not people, but property. Fifty years later, the United States Supreme Court ruled that for slaves who had been set free as people, *separate* educational institutions could be regarded as equality before the law. Now, one hundred years later, we are still working on many leftover problems! That fact, in itself, illustrates that the social order is not changed automatically "by changing individuals."

A second fallacy, involved in the assumption that the conversion of the individual will automatically change the world, lies in the fact that new Christians are described as "babes in Christ." A baby is complete in that he may have all of the necessary physical organs and bodily parts intact when he is born, but a baby is scarcely ready to assume his full social responsibilities. So new Christians are complete in terms of their new potentialities in Christ, but to provide for their development and use requires a whole lifetime. My personal conversion, therefore, may see me living for three decades with many unchristian attitudes, opinions, and unexamined assumptions which were formed before my conversion.

Our Christian mandate in evangelism involves both the personal and the social dimensions of human existence. As God's people, we seek to live and witness so as to bring others to a personal knowledge of Christ as Lord and Savior. As God's people, we invest ourselves also in bringing about needed changes in our social order which will help to humanize our life together and to bring the nations of the world into closer conformity with God's purposes in history.

If the evangelistic mission of the Christian church is so clearly perceived in its full dimensions, why is it that few churches appear to be effectively organized to implement the mission which Christ has given them?

We know from observation and experience that unconscious beliefs can shape our institutional structures and patterns of life and work. When, therefore, we see a church organizing its energies in ways which are contrary to its consciously professed convictions, we must conclude that its unexamined assumptions and beliefs are in the driver's seat, steering its institutional vehicle away from its announced goals. These unconscious assumptions, when examined more closely, often reflect the influence of Athens and its Hellenizing process which has colored Christian theology and practice. As a result, many aspects of Christian faith come to be understood as abstract ideals or as theoretical statements of metaphysics. For example, the word "faith," which in the biblical sense speaks both of the faithfulness of God and man's trusting relationship which leans on God, is changed to mean the acceptance of formal creeds or abstract dogmas. Enormous changes were effected in the church's life when Athens with its philosophical idealism prevailed over the biblical description of reality. Whereas man was understood in Hebraic terms as a living unity, he was divided into a spiritual essence living for a time in a material tomb called the "body." We hear it said, for example, that the church's business is "the saving of souls," and that this is the primary reason for the church's existence. We must affirm the accuracy of that statement *if* we think of the soul in biblical, rather than in Hellenistic terms of Platonic idealism. The soul is not something inside a man's material body which can be saved separately from the reality of man's whole existence. A soul is not just part of a man. According to the biblical account in Genesis, man becomes a living soul when he is fashioned by the creative hand of God as a whole person. Thus it is the whole man who is to share in the life of God through Christ and whose relationships are to be sustained and completed. Partly, this is why, as Christians, we believe that the Christian hope involves more than the old Grecian hope for the immortality of the soul. Our biblical hope speaks of nothing less than the resurrection of the body.

Our captivity to Athens has made it possible for us to define "spirituality" as a kind of immaterial idealism. But, the biblical witness speaks about the meaning of creation, asserting that God made all things, including matter, and called it good. A man is more than a disembodied spirit. The purpose of redemption is to fulfill God's original intent in creation and to restore what man in his perversity has marred, so that once again the material things of this world, together with man himself, might serve and glorify their Maker. The God of the Bible is a God of history, where, he tells us, he is working out his purposes. By defining spirituality in Hellenistic rather than in biblical terms, the church has too often suggested it wanted someone who would let the abyss of life alone, who would not disturb our comfortable, historical absenteeism which sees this world as a kind of anteroom where men wait until real life begins. We have forgotten the good news of the gospel that eternal life is God's gift to us here and now, that this *is* our Father's world, that the new age has already begun, even though hidden dimensions of its significance are not yet realized by men.

To be "spiritual" is to follow Christ as he seeks to lead men in the ways of truth, equity, justice, and righteousness, expressed in love of God and of neighbor. The Greeks believed that it was enough to put ideas into words to make them real. The Bible insists, as the First Letter of John states, we must put our love into deeds to make them real (cf. 1 John 3:18). Thus to be engaged in "the saving of souls" commits the church to be concerned about everything that limits, imprisons, and influences a man's life—for good or ill. Our evangelistic task, perceived in these terms, is to understand the cosmic reach and range of the love of Christ for the whole man and for the whole world. To be set free for its evangelistic mission, the church needs an exodus from Athens and the unexamined assumptions which have permitted us to neglect the biblical view of man which sees personality in its unitary aspects. This neglect has permitted us to embrace the Hellenistic view which sees man as a soul imprisoned in a body like a tomb.

At one time in his life, G. K. Chesterton was living in Battersea, a section of London. The story is told that as he was packing for a holiday trip and an extended vacation, a friend asked him where he was going. "To Battersea," Chesterton replied. "The wit of your remark escapes me," confessed his friend. "I," said Chesterton, "I'm going to Battersea via Paris, Heidelberg, Frankfurt. I am going to wander all over the world until once more I find Battersea. I cannot see any Battersea here, because a cloud of sleep and custom has come across my eyes. The only way to go to Battersea is to go away from it."

We are not asking the church to write a new gospel. But if the gospel itself is eternal, it comes to us in the familiar faces and pages and cadences of New Testament sounds and of the immediacy of our own Christian traditions. Many of us have long since grown accustomed to these familiar faces. We, like Chesterton, are blinded by a cloud of sleep and custom from perceiving the fullness of God's truth for us and our times. Only an exodus from our captivity to crippling unexamined assumptions can free the church to fulfill its evangelistic task.

4
An Exodus from Nicea

We have stated that the church is stalled in its evangelistic mission because of its bondage to unexamined assumptions stemming from Hellenistic metaphysical ideas. If we had thought we had been following Christ directly, we have discovered that because we have entertained the wrong ideas, as pictures in our heads, we have been following Jesus by way of Athens. Plato and Aristotle have long since died, but their influence lives after them. When man is understood as a rational thinker and truth is understood as contained in ideas, man's approach to God seems best achieved by thinking about God as an idea through a means and method of contemplation. The development of Western philosophy from Aristotle to Hegel was based on a gigantic fallacy, which turned abstract facts into spiritual essences, moved from history and nature to ideas and ideals. As a result, not only philosophical but also religious thinking has become a process of abstract rational thought no longer rooted in actual reality lived out amid the issues of time and history. Under this theory, people are changed, it is believed, by teaching them the right principles and then allowing them to apply those principles to life.

In this connection, Edwin Hatch observes a noticeable difference in the form and content between the Sermon on the Mount and the Nicene Creed. The Sermon on the Mount, he discovers, "assumes beliefs rather than formulates them; the theological conceptions which underlie it belong to the ethical rather than the speculative side of theology; metaphysics are wholly absent." In examining the Nicene Creed, to the contrary, he discovers it to be "a statement partly of historical facts and partly of dogmatic inferences; the metaphysical terms which it contains would probably have been unintelligible to the first disciples; ethics have no place in it."[1] The Sermon on the Mount belongs to a world of the Hebrew prophets, the Nicene Creed to a world of Greek philosophers.

Our problem in the church, as we have seen, is that we have been immobilized from personal and corporate action in behalf of our Christian mission because of our captivity to Athens. But we find ourselves in bondage also to Nicea. The church is seeking to minister in the twentieth century with creedal pictures that were framed in the first four centuries of Christian history. We not only have some of the wrong pictures in our heads, but we also have many of the wrong words on our lips. The church has been entrusted with a message and a ministry of reconciliation, but we have betrayed the message because we have misunderstood our ministry. The irony of our situation is that, living in a world where many means of communication are more readily available than ever, the church finds itself handicapped in communicating its message clearly and cogently.

A desk clerk at a motel received a long-distance phone call requesting an overnight reservation. The clerk asked the caller, "Would you like a room with a tub or a shower?" The caller replied, "What's the difference?" The clerk answered, "With a tub, you sit down!" The communications breakdown in this instance emerged from the fact that the clerk and the caller understood the word *"difference"* each in his own way. To the man calling, "difference" meant a variation in price. To the clerk, "difference" meant a variation in function. There was no "meeting of meanings" which must take place if communication is to involve the sharing of life as well as ideas. In all communications problems, there are "meaning barriers" which exist, focusing in language, images, anxieties, defenses, and purposes. One source has listed thirteen reasons for misunderstanding: (1) our experiences are different; (2) our perceptions of ourselves are different; (3) our images of others are different; (4) our needs and wants are different; (5) our values are different; (6) our problems are different; (7) our secrets are different; (8) our definitions are different; (9) our abilities to communicate are different; (10) our perceptions of expectations from others are different; (11) what we see is different; (12) we think others are like us; (13) misinterpretations of intermediaries cause misunderstanding.[2]

This helpful listing enables us to see that two men born in the same century, children of the same age, have difficulty in communicating to each other. The problem of the church in the communication of the Christian faith and gospel is intensified because it is in bondage to historic creeds which have been un-reformed in the continuing Christian experience in the life of a church. If we are to reach the men of our own generation, the miracle of Pentecost must happen all over again—when people hear in their own language the marvelous things which God has done for them in Jesus Christ. We need an exodus for the church from captivity in Nicea.

The late Samuel H. Miller was of the opinion that a radical split had opened up between the church and the world. In his words, "Something like a geological fault has happened, dropping the strata on one side far below the other, so they no longer meet. . . . The discontinuity is being felt on both sides, leaving the church stranded, and the world unsanctified." To support his thesis, he cited a word from Hendrik Kraemer, who charged that the church might just as well be using Egyptian hieroglyphics for all the understanding modern man has of its theological terms and jargon. In agreeing with Kraemer's conviction, Dr. Miller commented that the vocabulary of the church turns out to be "a special vocabulary for a special place, like the auctioneer's chant at a tobacco sale."[3]

J. V. Langmead Casserley writes in a substantiating fashion when he reminds us that "we are living through a time of profound historical change and social crisis in which men find it more and more difficult to enter into the symbolic inheritance characteristic of the societies to which they belong."[4] One practical result of this general alienation from traditional social symbols of earlier generations is that the Christian evangelist finds himself in a somewhat similar predicament. The symbolic language upon which he must depend to communicate the substance of the Christian faith also turns out to be part of a similar symbolic inheritance from which contemporary society is estranged. However, the church does not face the task of inventing an entirely new language. Casserley points out that it is a paradox that "we can only say new things in a world in which men go on saying old things, for to assert the old things is not merely to reassert them but also to keep alive the language in terms of which the new things can intelligibly be said."[5]

This point may be illustrated by the long-distance trunk lines which take many voices and scramble the words in new combinations of electrical impulses as they speed along the circuits much faster than the sound of each separate word. But, on the other end, the new world of electronic communication has to unscramble the sounds and to restore the individual words so that the listener can hear what the caller has to say. Thus if in the church the evangelist or the witness succeeds only in scrambling the traditional sounds of the gospel, he will be heard, but not understood. For the church to have a usable future, it must have a usable past which contains enough intelligible continuity to bridge the gaps between generations and the culture of church and world.

To recognize the need for an exodus from the classical creeds produced in the first four centuries of the Christian faith is to recognize that these creeds were themselves the product of the metaphysical questions which were raised by the real men living in that period of human history. These were real questions, and the statements and formulations in response to them represented real struggles. But the truth is that the situation with man today is not the same. The questions of modern man are no longer phrased in metaphysical terms, but in political, economic, social, and psychical terms. We cannot, as a church, hope to hear these contemporary questions, let alone to regard them as real, if we impose upon them and their hearers the arbitrary solutions and formulations of earlier centuries. The twentieth century must be as free to follow the leading and the guiding of the Spirit of God as was the first century or the third or the sixteenth. There is far too much pertinence in the criticism made by L. P. Jacks when he says:

> We have cooped up the faith in theological fortresses, surrounding it with an immense array of outworks—creeds, dogmas, apologetics, institutions—and we have used up our resources in holding our "positions" against one another when we ought to have been attacking the common enemy in the open field.[6]

Also, John Oman does not believe that we can shut up the power of the living God in any of our definitions. He says, "Sometimes they sum it all up as a fixed physical order, and call themselves scientists; sometimes as a fixed rational order, and call themselves philosophers." But Oman saves his most withering scorn for those "who sum it up as a fixed spiritual order, whom we call ecclesiastics. . . ." [7]

Considering the crippling bondage of the church to its unreformed creeds, we must be willing to "switch rather than fight." The word for heresy in the New Testament comes from *hairesis*, which was, at the outset, a neutral word meaning "to choose." Later it came to mean "a party or a school of thought, a sect, or a faction." In the New Testament, the same Greek word is used of the Sadducees (Acts 5:17). It is also used to describe the Pharisees (Acts 15:5). On four other occasions, it is the word used by antagonistic Jews to describe Christians. Any man who had a different view, or who belonged to a different school, or party, was "a heretic." Because we do not believe that there is any one infallible interpretation of the Bible, because we do not have one officially received creed, and because we do not have the luxury of an external authority which has the last word for our faith and practice, the church and the believers in it, under the guidance of God's Spirit, must be granted room to stand, to search, and to grow in the life of Christian faith. The words of Jesus are as applicable to us today as they were when they were first spoken to his disciples. "I have yet many things to say to you, but you cannot bear them now" (John 16:12). It is our loyalty to Jesus Christ and his continuing leadership through the Spirit which demands the liberty of an exodus which allows us to amend and to enrich our earlier confessions and statements of faith.

Because we believe that all truth is of God, Christians at their best have proved willing to leave their house of bondage and to follow that counsel which says that we must sit down with the wide-eyed expectancy of a child before a new fact can speak to us. If that represents good counsel for the empirical sciences, it represents also helpful guidance if Christian faith is to become personal rather than merely propositional, experiential as well as historical. No less a person than Jonathan Edwards, despite all of his tradition, observed that as men grow older, they, like institutions, tend to become entrenched by their old habits of thought. As a result, they screen out new and promising discoveries.

No man can read the New Testament with sensitive insight without seeing that the impact of Jesus upon the life of the world was his insistence that each man in every generation is to rethink the meaning of God and to give statement to his discoveries and experience. Jesus stands against the sin of the closed mind and the finished creed. A university pastor made this point clearly in an annual sermon addressed to a religious gathering. He said:

Our family has several neighbors who have children the age of my seven-year-old son. Some of these children had begun their catechism classes at their church. One day the kids were sparring at each other across the backyard fence, and one of the girls said to my son, "Polly is better than you are, because she knows *all* about

God!" And my son responded very simply and very innocently, "Nobody knows *all* about God." How better can you state the Protestant principle? And how we papas and mamas need to remember that! [8]

To speak of "the Protestant principle" reminds us of the provisional nature of all our creeds and theological statements as well as our institutions. The Protestant principle emerges from the fact of God's self-disclosure in the historic life of Jesus but includes also the continuing self-disclosure in the Christ of faith. It is our faith that the event of Christ could not be exhausted or depleted in his own generation or his own century. In Christ, men have unique accessibility to God. In the words of Edwin Lewis:

> Christ is permanently the way to God. But he could not be that if he had remained merely a historical figure. We have to go back to the records to know certain things about him, but the Christian does not approach God through a record, not even through a record so incomparable as that of the New Testament. He approaches God, as the author of the Epistle to the Hebrews says, by "a new and living way." [9]

Hence, the Living Word is more than a book lying on the pulpit in church, or on the living room table at home, waiting passively for the initiative of human hands to open it, deliver it, expound it, and carry it into the life of the world. The gospel is life and not a dead letter. Because the Word of God is living, it cannot be bound. If men could not succeed in making Jesus' tomb a prison, we should be surprised if either a church or a creed, a liturgy or a ritual, a building or a book, a dogma or a discipline, a definition or a denomination, could succeed in containing his limitless life and power in any set of religious creeds, however venerated they may be in our thinking. When the Word became flesh in the incarnation, God signified to us that his highest revelation comes not in the right words, but in the right deeds; not in doctrinal formulas, but in a devoted fellowship; not in final principles, but in a final Person. Words change with the passing of time. Hence, if we confuse the gospel with the words that were used either in the fourth century or the first century, we tend to limit its range and power. Some persons insist that the gospel is a faith once for all delivered to the saints in correct propositional form, because they believe that this is the only way to keep the gospel safe from contamination and change. But they must face the paradox that, by insisting on their unreformed creeds and descriptions, they hasten the very process which they fear and seek to delay.

D. M. Baillie illustrates this very fact when he says:

> The attempt to put our experience of God into theological statements is something like the attempt to draw a map of the world on a flat surface, the page of an atlas. It is impossible to do this without a certain degree of falsification, because the surface of the earth is a spherical surface whose pattern cannot be reproduced accurately upon a plane. And yet the map must be drawn for convenience' sake.[10]

It is because we confess, with Paul, that we have not yet attained or that we have not yet been made perfect and that we see as through a glass darkly, that we recognize the need for continued growth and for the freedom to change our minds and our creeds. Such an awareness is not only a matter of intellectual integrity and honesty, it is an essential requirement if the church is to be able to bear witness powerfully and meaningfully to the Christian faith to the men of its own generation. In Orwell's *Nineteen Eighty-Four,* a friend of Winston Smith speaks to him from his position in the Research Department in the Ministry of Truth,

> We're getting the language into its final shape—the shape it's going to have when nobody speaks anything else. . . .
>
> Don't you see that the whole aim of Newspeak is to narrow the range of thought? In the end we shall make thoughtcrime [an individual idea which differs from propaganda issued by the Ministry of Truth] literally impossible.... Every concept that can ever be needed will be expressed by exactly *one* word, with its meaning rigidly defined and all its subsidiary meanings rubbed out and forgotten. . . . Every year fewer and fewer words, and the range of consciousness always a little smaller. . . . Orthodoxy means not thinking—not needing to think![11]

This chilling picture, which portrays the dehumanizing power of the totalitarian state, offers us a graphic illustration of what takes place in the life of a church when words are no longer renewed and refreshed in the present experience of men but become used as empty slogans and fixed stereotypes. To the contrary, wherever Jesus comes in his ministry, his Gospel humanizes, liberates, and fructifies. His methods are not dull and stereotyped, but dynamic and fertile. He healed several blind men, according to the record, but never exactly in the same way or with the same words, as if deliberately to teach us that there is no *one* simple formula which, automatically repeated, makes the unseen world our servant, an Aladdin rubbing his genie lamp. Jesus told one man that he must be born again. However, according to the records, that is the only instance in which he used those words, as if to suggest that the secret passes which lead into the human heart are never exactly the same in every person. In nature, it is God who produces the river; it is man who makes the canal. In religion, how have we fallen into the error that God's method involves only the canal with its even measurements of our religious creeds and formularies? The historic genius for a free conscience is never closer to the spirit of the New Testament than when it insists that religious confessions and creeds may be accepted as testimonies, but they cannot be imposed as tests upon the current generation to measure, control, or communicate a vital and authentic Christian experience.

A new exodus from Nicea is needed for the church to free it from captivity to earlier, unreformed and unrenewed creeds and statements. The church must have freedom and flexibility to follow the light in order to fulfill its evangelistic mission in letting God speak through our common life in the vernacular of our own century. As Jesus pointed out to the religious leaders of his own day, they could not find life poring over the sacred writings; they must come to him if they were to have life. (See John 6:39.) The apostle Paul's own confession of faith does not read, "I know what I believe" but "I know whom I have believed" (2 Timothy 1:12). Growing companionship with the Spirit of Christ constantly enlarges and enriches the *what* of our faith so that it is changed from faith to faith and cannot be understood as a rigid body of fixed and static dogmas. However. a discerning writer reminds us that new truth, which is to say, our fresh and larger experience of an old truth, never comes to us like the grocer adding one more can of beans to others on his shelf. Instead, it is more like the farmer who adds a new field to his farm. The "new" truth usually shifts existing boundaries. The threat of such a change often tempts us to meet an unfamiliar truth with a shotgun in our hands and an unfriendly look upon our faces. We should not wonder that many of the people we hope to evangelize are scared off before they come within range of our voices.

Several years ago I was dumbfounded to read a report in one of our weekly news magazines that most of our United States envoys in the Middle East at that time had a severe language handicap because only a handful of them spoke Arabic. The news report went on to say that, according to the facts released by the United States Office of Education, nearly half of the nation's entire diplomatic corps had no useful grasp of any foreign language. Naïvely, I had assumed that one of the first requirements for a person to represent our nation abroad would be an understanding of the culture and a usable facility in the language of the country to which the American ambassador was being sent. While pondering what the handicap might mean to our State Department and our foreign policy, I was led also to conjecture about our inability to communicate the gospel effectively in the evangelization of the world. Inheriting our religious concepts as much from Greece as from the Bible, and our creeds and hymns from earlier centuries, the church has sought to keep its symbols alive by refreshing and restoring them in the life of its own church membership. This very process has increased the distance between professed Christian people and their neighbors. Without a useful grasp of the language of the contemporary world into which we are sent as ambassadors for Christ, we are unable either to understand or to be understood. We desperately need symbols of communication which are rooted in our common human experience rather than in a restricted and specialized "religious" experience. The early church did this when, with the gospel in their hands, they borrowed the Greek koiné, the common language of the man in the street as the vehicle for their expression. The absence of the poor or the rich, the black or the brown or the white, the children or the youth or the aged, the absence of the power structures of the community or the disen-franchised—the absence of these groups and persons from the life of the church often results in the church talking to itself. God does not intend the message of the church to be restricted to its members, as though the church were a closed corporation with dividends to be voted only to its stockholders. Instead, as a public service corporation, existing for the life of the world, the church must be led out of bondage through the Red Sea which has served as a com-munications moat, separating God's people as ambassadors from the life of the world where they are to be sent.

5
An Exodus from Jerusalem

When he wrote his *Secular City,* Harvey Cox confessed:

> . . . there are certain matters in which the only productive relationship must be disaffiliation. It may be that the debilitating institution-centered thinking of churches is not something that can be corrected wholly "from within." The problem with denominational organizations is not that they have splendid institutional apparatus that is simply being used in the wrong way. If this were the case, then a minor palace insurrection in denominational headquarters might win the day.[1]

However, Cox identifies the problem as of a much deeper nature, so that even the most progressive or prophetic leadership soon finds itself faltering "under the weight of the massive institutional determinants with which it must work." [2] In the years which have elapsed since he wrote those words, there is little evidence that would modify our feeling that the church is in captivity to its institutional intractability and its resistance to change.

Numerous critics have pointed out that the traditional residential patterns of the parish indicate that their organizational life is based upon sociological patterns which prevailed before automobiles, labor unions, shift work, and other urban and industrial patterns were developed. The first-century church could be described as one which looked forward in eager faith for the fulfillment of God's promise in the Lord's return. The twentieth-century church, unfortunately, looks back to the first century, or some period since then, to explain its present institutional life and organization. At the outset, in the life of the early church, we find the disciples trapped in Jerusalem behind closed doors because of the pressure of their fears. But, under the pressure of God's presence by his Spirit and the outward circumstances of persecution, we see the church slowly adapting and adjusting itself to its environment. From the framework of Jewish exclusivism, one can trace the growth of the church as it moves to the Samaritan world and, ultimately, establishes a new center in Antioch for its further expansion in the Gentile world. The first meetings are within the framework of the established synagogues and reflect a strong sense of nationalism, but gradually we see the patterns being adjusted to the emerging environment.

In Ephesians, Paul affirms that all walls have been abolished and abrogated in Jesus Christ. The church that insists on shutting itself away from the life of the world behind brick and mortar, seeking shelter and security, is trusting in an illusion. We need to be wary of the fate of the lobster which, for the sake of immunity, got itself into a coat of mail and has stayed in its prison ever since. Healthy organisms do not think of their processes, but of their purposes. The preoccupation of the contemporary church, seeking to find security in its bondage, rather than flexibility and the risk of freedom in its mission, suggests how deeply the roots of institutional idolatry have planted themselves in our contemporary soil. The church needs a new exodus from Jerusalem which stands as the symbol of the temple of the Lord which does not save. Historians have traced the death of many notable civilizations because of their rigidity and inflexibility. Faced with new crises and challenges, they woodenly repeated their earlier responses. But in changed circumstances and conditions, these responses proved no longer adequate.

In much the same way, the modern church is hampered by its rigid, ecclesiastical blueprints which we believe someone has dug up from the ruins of the early church. We fail to see that what made the first-century church authentic and dynamic was its own response to its own century. This response involved many religious innovations and required disloyalty and discontinuity with past traditions. Alfred N. Whitehead warns us that any society which wishes to avoid the inner decay of atrophy, or the catastrophic convulsions of anarchy, must learn to combine reverence for its traditional symbols with freedom for their revision.[3] In our case, what is required for the church to be faithful to its worldwide mission is nothing less than exodus from its institutional shelters so that we may follow Christ "outside the camp" (cf. Hebrews 13:12). Our exodus takes us outside the walls where the church affirms not its separateness but its solidarity with the world. We aim with a transcendent grace for an open society in which God is free to work as it pleases him and where we are receptive to the further light which breaks forth from his Word to judge and to renew the present patterns of our Christian mission.

Our exodus is to the frontiers of human need as we prove willing to leave fixed and settled positions to follow Christ's Spirit in new paths, assured that we in the twentieth century have the same resources and options which were open to the first-century church because we, too, have stepped into the same new age which, by faith, is as near to us today as it was to first-century Christians. This concern for flexibility and freedom reflects the primary premise of our free church position. We affirm that the living God is free, having an unconditioned essence and existence. Pioneers in religious freedom understood that God's freedom demanded a free church and Bible and a person who was free to respond and to believe for himself. They insisted that the Bible be unchained from the pulpit where it had been accessible to the official priest or minister alone. They were anxious to have the Book phrased in the popular tongue and placed in the hands of all believers. They reasoned that God must be allowed to speak directly to each man's conscience. They insisted that only a free church provided the propitious climate where the spontaneity and diversity of God's Spirit could freely encounter and claim men in their personal response of faith and commitment. Like the wind, which no man is able to control or manipulate, they sensed that the living Spirit of God is free to choose the manner and the method, the place and the person, the symbol and the sacrament, the sermon and the Scripture, and the season and the song where he makes his presence known. The struggle for religious liberty and freedom of conscience, which was pursued by many Christians, emerged as a corollary to the primary premise that God is free.

In the formative years of our experience as a people of God, believers in the emerging Reformation insisted that the church must claim the right and responsibility to reform its life in the light of Scripture and the leading and guidance of God's Spirit. The institutions of the church, after the second century, were formed within the framework of the Roman Empire, so that the church's traditional, institutional life came to reflect the social and political framework of the empire with its provinces, senate, and imperial government. The structure of the organized church today carries this reflected organizational basis of the political systems which were accidental to Christianity and which had intrinsically nothing to do with it. Carlyle Marney put it bluntly when he said that while the principles of faith may be regarded as eternal, it is necessary to let the expressions of faith change so that they can develop and find new forms and expressions. He concludes: "The vehicle, the carriage, the bucket, the cup, the glass, the container"—these are not essential parts of the faith itself. Without a willingness "to remodel the wagon, to overhaul the chassis, without the Protestant principle of critical reevaluation of our institutional bases, religion dies. Young men and women walk away from its sagging structures in globs." [4]

In most religions there has been an attempt to preserve the conditions under which the religion began because these conditions have seemed to be an essential part of the religion. However, the Christian faith has the potential, which has often been demonstrated, to be a fermenting principle of change in society. At its best, the Christian faith is centered in a person and a spirit, rather than in a proposition or code of law and ritual. Christ has entrusted the church to shape its life in response to the guidance of his Spirit. His continuing Presence offers flexibility, vitality, and freedom for the life and mission of the church.

Unfortunately, the very lack of vitality and flexibility for mission and for the use of new evangelistic methods militates against the ability of the contemporary church to cope with the rapid changes of its own environment. Some may believe that the patterns of church organization are infallibly laid down in biblical command and precedent. Thus, some read the account of Acts 6 and conclude that the pattern and precedent afforded us in this example is that: (1) every church should have officers called deacons; (2) they should be seven in number: and (3) they should have Grecian names. Instead, can we not conclude with equal authority that the precedent suggests the need for the church to meet new problems with a prayerful and a progressive spirit? Faithfulness to follow Christ's leading requires freedom and flexibility. Watching the birds of the season in their annual migrations, Jeremiah (cf. Jeremiah 8:7, Moffatt) reasoned that the birds of the air have instinct and obedience enough to follow the changing seasons, knowing that migration would lead not to their extinction but to their life. But he saw a strange callous disregard on the part of God's people to the Eternal's laws and to their contemporary situation and its meaning.

A crippling flexibility gap still exists in the instincts and experience of the institutional church so that we still seek shelter and security in the wrong places and from the wrong hands. One is reminded of the man aboard ship in the middle thirties. A number of persons sitting in their steamer deck chairs were talking about the rise of Adolf Hitler and the threat of the Nazi party on the continent of Europe and the possible dangers which might engulf the

Western world in another war. One of the men in the center of the conversation took a well-worn map from his pocket, opened it, and showed his friends a secluded island to which he said he and his family would go for refuge in the event of such a war. The name of the island in the Pacific was Okinawa! Ask any marine who was there in the middle forties if that was an adequate place to hide!

History reveals that whenever the church insists on hiding, the world becomes an instrument in God's hand to liberate the church from its false shelters and its institutional idolatries. This conclusion is not unrelated to a view of the prophetic office in which the prophet can be seen as an idol smasher. He insists on living outside the institutional structure himself and will have none of its security and safety in order that he may speak against it. When American churches are in a billion-dollar building boom, the Bible reminds us that if the heaven of heavens cannot contain God, how much less any of the buildings which we build for him today (cf. 1 Kings 8:27). When the people are saying "the temple of the Lord," the prophet's voice will thunder, "The temple of the Lord, it cannot save." (Cf. Jeremiah 7:3-4.) These words support those who believe that when God spoke about building a house, he was thinking of a holy people rather than a holy place, so that the temple of the Lord would be his people gathered or scattered, who would diffuse the knowledge of the living God throughout the whole wide earth.

But we must understand that the purpose of the prophet's voice is not simply to tear down. God demolishes our false shelters and our institutional idolatry. He seeks to lead us from our captivity in Jerusalem in order that he may build up. God calls us to discard accumulated baggage so that we begin a pilgrimage of faith afresh. In a day when many young people and others are turned off by bureaucracy and by institutional structures, we cannot forget that the Christian faith began because Jesus Christ came into history in bodily form. The New Testament sees the church functioning as the body of Christ. The Gnostic heresy of the late first century denied the bodily reality of Jesus in his incarnation. Like Alice, in *Adventures Through the Looking Glass,* who met a Cheshire cat which disappeared leaving only its grin, we can't dispense with the real history of the church with its victories and losses across the centuries. Institutional structures are devices that free us as individuals from the endless and frustrating process of having to learn everything by ourselves through trial and error. Institutions do not need to be dehumanizing, but they can enable us to draw upon accumulated resources of human social experience. In this way, institutions are time-saving as well as time-binding. We are weary of the repetitious criticisms which imply that the church is not meant to be "the body of Christ" needing therefore bodily form and structure.

The necessary corrective may be found in the words adopted by delegates at the Whitby Assembly of the International Missionary Council when they said: "The whole church must brace itself to face the frontier.... It must become a mobile missionary force.... It is a time for us all to be thinking of campaign tents, rather than of cathedrals."

If the Lord God did not like the noise of ancient solemn assemblies, which ignored the cause of the poor and needy and overlooked social injustices and oppression, and if he revealed (Isaiah 58) the kind of a fast which would please him, how have we managed to convince ourselves that, apart from some basic change in God's character, he could be pleased with the sound of our church meetings and the captivity of our institutional structures which show a modern church not only in suburban captivity but in easy conformity with its culture and on good terms with Herod, Pilate, Caiaphas, and every other force which nailed Jesus to his cross? If the gospel is meant to be seed, we must not regard it as though it were an institutional hothouse plant; if it is light, we must not hide it under the bushel of our church roof; if it is salt, we must not try to keep it safe in unshaken, ecclesiastical containers; if it is yeast, we must mix it with the whole mass of dough which heavily awaits a leavening!

James Baldwin has a plaintive description in his novel, *Go Tell It on the Mountain,* of a boy who frequented the New York City main public library. He was drawn to the building because of the stone lions that stand on guard. Although he was a member of the Harlem branch library and was entitled to take books from the big library itself, he had never ventured inside. The halls seemed too vast, the building too big. He was afraid he would get lost or make some blunder upon entering which would subject him to either pity or scorn. He always rationalized that he would enter some other day, when he had mastered other books uptown and his feelings as well.[5]

In a sense Baldwin was describing the manner in which a great group of young people and unchurched people in contemporary society view our institutional structures and forms in the life of the church as an alien culture. They are led to reject the church as an institution, not so much because they are not hungry for the reality to which it points, but because they feel that the institution with its resistance to change is rejecting them. Unless the church is able to experience an exodus from its captivity, in the very act of prolonging its further institutional existence, we face the danger that our conditions may become so rigid that they will choke and kill the living spirit which brought them forth.

Most of us have observed some phase of business which has been eclipsed because of the inability on the part of its leaders to cope with its changing environment and with the necessary development of new markets. For example, advocates and manufacturers of the steam engine in the railroad business could not envision the day when the steam engine would be eclipsed by diesels. In 1935 a vice-president of one of the major locomotive works said:

> We are having quite a ballyhoo about streamlined, lightweight trains and diesel locomotives, and it is no wonder the public feels that the steam locomotive is about to lay down and play dead. Yet over the years certain simple fundamental principles continue to operate. Some time in the future, when all this is reviewed, we will not find our railroads any more dieselized than they are electrified.[6]

Three years later, the chief executive of a major manufacturing competitor to this vice-president's firm said, "For a century, as you know, steam has been the principal railroad . . . power. It still is and, in my view, will continue to be." [7] While these famous last words were being made by executives who refused to recognize emerging facts, other manufacturing companies were acquiring more than 75 percent of the railroad locomotive business, and their new diesel engines were destined to send steam engines to many of the city parks around the nation as relics of the distant past.

We may be further surprised to learn that while Aristotle was lecturing in Athens, one of his pupils, Alexander the Great, was leading his armies in conquest of the known world, marching off all the existing maps. However, Aristotle was still thinking and philosophizing in terms of the little, independent, autonomous city-states of Greece, small enough to hear the voice of the herald and for each citizen to participate in the public realm. Thus, the greatest thinker of his time failed to see in the rise of the Macedonian Empire the dawning of a new era which was destined to bring profound changes to the Hellenistic political scene and to the existing structures of Athenian society. While human leadership remains an essential resource in the life of the church, we need a wisdom beyond our own to see the shape of things to come and to gain courage and strength to follow the pillar of cloud by day and the pillar of fire by night from our institutional captivity to the acceptance and the fulfillment of our mission.

"Which mountain?" asked the woman of Samaria. "Which place is the right place for us to worship and settle down?" Jesus answered, "Neither mountain, nor place, for 'God is spirit and those who worship him must worship in spirit and truth' " (cf. John 4:19-24). His future disciples were to discover that a man could be as close to God in Calgary as at Calvary, as close to God in Joppa as in Jerusalem, as close to God in Bethlehem, Pennsylvania, as in Bethlehem of Judea. Both the pattern and the dynamic for a new exodus for the church from its institutional bondage is summarized by the message of the angel outside the empty tomb of Jesus, " 'He has been raised from death, and now he is going ahead of you. . . .' So they left the grave in a hurry, afraid and yet filled with joy, and ran to tell his disciples" (See Matthew 28:7-8, TEV). The risen Spirit of Jesus can deliver the church from its desire to safeguard its existence and to preserve its immunity in its institutional shelters and idolatries. More than that, we can be spared the fatal blunder of planning for yesterday instead of tomorrow in the light of today. Apart from such an exodus, we will fail to achieve what one management consultant has called "the management of Perpetuity with the management of Innovation." Without such an exodus, we will go on building hitching posts for automobiles.

6
An Exodus from Rome

We have been saying that the church in America is in trouble because of its resistance to change due to its institutional bondage and structural rigidity and captivity. It is in trouble and there is an exodus from the church because it has adopted what Walt Kelly once described as "a frog's eye-view of the world." [1] Kelly noted that when a frog stands up to look into his future path, the place and the shape of his eyes permit him to see only the way he has already taken. Looking back at the selfsame road he has already traversed, he believes himself nonetheless to be looking forward and mistakenly assumes that the road ahead is not different from the road behind him. The church is in trouble because it has become preoccupied with the task of saving and serving its own organizational life, despite the warning of Jesus that "he who seeks to save his life will lose it" (cf. Mark 8:35). Spending all of its energies in its fight for institutional identity and existence, the church is like an oil refinery that does not require any marketing or sales department nor any barrels or pipeline for shipment of its products because the refinery consumes all of the oil it refines.

The church is in trouble because it lacks the capacity for adaptability and flexibility so that it has been unable to respond to its changing environment. The church suffers because, in many dimensions of its life and work, it is functioning without either the understanding or the consent of the public. In his book *Only by Public Consent*, L. L. L. Golden makes an important point unmistakably clear. He says:

> The lessons for corporations are clear and unmistakable. They cannot function without public consent. To obtain that consent they must act in the public interest as the public interprets it at any given time. On the day that management forgets that an institution cannot continue to exist if the general public feels that it is not useful, or that it is anti-social in the public concept of what is anti-social, the institution will begin to die. . . .
>
> Public consent does not stem from gimmicks or tricks. It exists because of performance in the public interest—plus . . . explaining to the public what an organization is doing and why.[2]

One cannot read such comments without seeing their application to a church. When the general public decides that an organized church in a given community or an established denomination is no longer functioning in the public interest, that church and that denomination begin to cumber the ground. During the decade of the sixties, the church in America lost several important spheres of Christian influence because, to a large degree, it failed to win the understanding or to gain the public consent of millions of youth and adults who concluded that the church was serving its own institutional life rather than serving the public interests. Men are reluctant to break off any relationship or to let any institution or organization to which they belong decline and die if they deem its existence important to their own well-being and to their future.

Yet the operation of this very principle creates a sense of crisis within the life of a church. One of the factors which has militated against the effective service of the church in America is that it has been taken into cultural captivity. It has been so responsive to national values that the church has lost its transcendent dimensions of grace and gospel. The church will be Christian because what it has to say, in terms of its evangelistic message, transcends the public values of any single community in any given age. It is at the point of its transcendence that the church may face rejection and hostility because its word or its action or its ministry appears to be *against* the public interest, unpatriotic and un-American. Caught in the tension of conflicting expectations, the church has often betrayed the universal and ultimate in the Christian message by being national, local, and too American.

The relationships between church and state, religion and patriotism, remain as vexing problems in our contemporary American life and pertain quite critically to the ability of the church to win men to a commitment of life to Jesus Christ which matches the willingness of the early disciples to stand against the power of the state, whether it was represented by King Herod or by the Roman Caesar. To regain its freedom for authentic Christian witness, which is able to win men to an unreserved faith and obedience in Jesus Christ, the church must experience an exodus from its cultural captivity symbolized by Rome in the first century and by the national capitols of our own century.

In considering the cultural captivity of the church, let us confess that it is not easy to arrive at a simplistic formula which satisfies every contemporary occasion. When we go back to the Bible or to the practices of the early church, we see diversity at work rather than uniformity. In the Old Testament, one may cite the counsel of the prophet Isaiah when he led his nation in a strong resistance movement to military oppression from outside the nation. On the other hand, another person may choose Jeremiah as his authority, who preached collaboration with the enemy rather than resistance. Both prophets claim to be speaking for God, even though in differing periods of their national history. Their counsel to the nation seems to be contradictory. Or, in the New Testament, one may quote a passage like, "Let every person be subject to the governing authorities" (Romans 13:1). This text seems to support an appeal for law and order. However, another person may choose to quote the familiar lines of Peter and the apostles, "We must obey God rather than men" (Acts 5:29). This text supports the man who desires to follow the pressure of his conscience in civil protest and disobedience, believing that he is obeying the higher moral law of God over against an invalid or unjust decree of man.

When Jesus was hailed before Pilate, the accusation made against him was "We caught this man misleading our people, telling them not to pay taxes to the Emperor and claiming that he himself is Christ, a king" (Luke 23:2, TEV). When Pilate sought to release Jesus, his adversaries insisted, "He is starting a riot among the people with his teaching!" (Luke 23:5, TEV). The charge brought against Jesus, which led to his death, was that he had spoken against the nation. He was unpatriotic! He had spoken against the established law. He had upset tradition. He had spoken against the temple. He was the enemy of organized religion. In much the same way, in the Roman Empire early Christians were accused of being atheists because they did not render their pinch of incense on the altar and permit Christ to be placed in the Roman Pantheon—one god among many.

The record makes it plain that Jesus did not refuse to render tax to Caesar. He was willing for men to give to the state what belonged to the state, but he was unwilling, either for himself or for others, to be required to give to the state what belongs to God. In *Nineteen Eighty-Four,* George Orwell sees this point in the tensions and conflict which surround Winston Smith amid the pressures of the totalitarian state. His problem was that "Big Brother," the totalitarian state, demanded more than external support. Smith is informed by his accusers and his tormentors, "It is not enough to obey [Big Brother]; you must love him." [3] The state became idolatrous because it refused to let Smith keep his heart or his conscience inviolate. He was coerced into surrendering his inward loyalty. The ultimate concern which belongs to God alone, as Sovereign and undivided Lord of the human conscience, can never be the proper province of any government or any state. Thus, in the life of Jesus, his lack of patriotism, in that he would not regard his civil obligations as absolute, led to Pilate's reluctant decision. The fact that Jesus had spoken against his own nation as a Jew appeared to be of small concern to the Roman governor. He had watched and heard many endless religious quarrels and controversy. But when the accusers of Jesus asserted that he had spoken against Caesar, Pilate, whose role as governor was to maintain the peace of the Roman Empire in the province, had second thoughts. Where Caesar is sovereign and where the state is worshiped, no one can refuse to offer his heart without facing condemnation. It is significant to note that Jesus was crucified, the Roman punishment meted out to criminals, and especially to seditious leaders who were regarded as having acted against the unity of the empire.

What does Jesus' experience and example say to us as Christians today? The simplest statement we must make is that God has not changed since the first century. If he refused to divide his sovereignty with Caesar then, we can conclude that Jesus does not divide his sovereignty now. If the demands of Caesar for inward affection were idolatrous then, the demand to make any national government lord of the conscience is likewise idolatrous now. In the conflict between the expectations of the social order and the private conscience, the confession of Simon Peter appears to stand unchallenged and unchanged. Christians must give to God what belongs to God, while they give to the state what belongs to it. But we would be in error to assume that God and the state stand as co-equals. When men are caught in the tension between the demands of God and the demands of the state, it is apparent that they must obey God rather than men. The things which belong to Caesar are limited and conditional; loyalty and obedience to Christ must be freely and unconditionally given. When the cross and the flag collide, men in the life of the church must be free to say, "Jesus, I my cross have taken, all to leave and follow Thee."

Such a confession of conscience, we acknowledge, is filled with many risks. The conscience of any man may only be half formed, or ill-formed, and is, therefore, a very fallible instrument which can lead a man amiss. No man, therefore, should find it easy to decry the claims of patriotism. When we hear the roll of drums and the call of the bugle, when our national flag symbolizes the best of our national ideals, when we read the roll call of our national heroes and remember their valor which has provided us space to think our thoughts, form our relationships, and claim our freedom, we can never be unmindful of what we owe to those who spilled their devotion in our behalf. But we must also know the meaning of that line on the London monument to Edith Cavell, who spent herself in tireless devotion to her country and then at the close of her life was led to say, "Patriotism is not enough." Great and good as patriotism is, it is not enough because no government is good enough to be loved. No system of politics is perfect enough to be embraced blindly. No national policy is so infallible that it cannot be questioned. No elected official is so absolute that he can be followed without some limit on our fealty. As great as America has been and is to us who are her sons and daughters, she is not divine. We do our nation no service if we withhold our critical judgment as loyal citizens, if we provide no room for honest dissent, if we know that what we owe to God, the Lord alone of conscience, we can never surrender to the state.

Often we are told that a man's personal problems can be solved if only he will come closer to Christ, or the church's impotence and weakness can be overcome if the church comes closer to Christ. But to honor that appeal means that we must come closer to his way of thinking, to his outlook about both God and man, and to his scale of values about the meaning of life. To be closer to Christ means that we must be willing to adjust, to change, to grow, and to be willing to be unadjusted to the present age and its cultural values because we are more adjusted to the ages. To be closer to Christ and to his way of thinking and his way of life may involve us in the heresy of being "un-American."

But to know what is "un-American," we must agree first of all on what is American. Who sets the standard? Who defines for us what is American so that we can know for all time henceforth what and who are the un-Americans? A review of our national history reveals that, in such a pluralistic society, the answers to these questions have changed with the passing of the years. When Massachusetts had an established church, religious freedom was un-American. Before the Emancipation Proclamation, human freedom for black men was un-American. Since the adoption of the Fourteenth Amendment, slavery and human servitude are un-American. Before the adoption of the Nineteenth Amendment, universal women's suffrage was un-American. Every woman reading this book would have been un-American had she attempted to vote. Since the triumph of women's suffrage, the right to vote for women became as American as apple pie. When the Volstead Act was ratified, legalized liquor was pronounced un-American. Now, because "beer belongs," teetotaling temperance people are un-American. When America signed the Kellogg-Briand Peace Pact, militarism was un-American; in more recent years, amid the conflict of Southeast Asia, pacifism is un-American. And thousands of young people have sought refuge for their consciences in other lands. In the time of the first League of Nations, international responsibility was un-American. When we entered the United Nations, isolationism had become un-American.

Thus, to be closer to Jesus Christ and his way of thinking about the world and the kingdom of God and the places where they collide means that the church, in the proclamation of its message, may appear to many persons as "un-American." We have already pointed out that his un-Jewish activities led Jesus to the cross. His un-Roman activities led the apostle Paul to prison. He was charged with advocating customs which his accusers said were not lawful for them as Romans to receive or follow. This has been the history of the people of God whose faith transcends all national ties and boundaries of a given period of human history amid the pressures of a single culture. When Abraham became the pilgrim of faith, his un-Sumerian activities led him to move out and made him the instrument of God's purpose. When Moses and his people fulfilled the promise of God, it required un-Egyptian activities for them to obey God's voice and to find their exodus. When Jeremiah prophesied against armed resistance to Babylon, it was by these un-Judean activities that he sought to save his nation from utter destruction. During the Nazi tyranny, there were but a few voices in Germany whose un-Aryan activities sought to speak to the meaning of God's purpose in behalf of a Christian faith that transcended the national goals of the German government. Because Jesus Christ does transcend all national and all denominational ties, to be closer to him in his way of thinking and to his outlook will require us at many points to appear unadjusted to our culture and to local customs and to become un-American in relation to established national traditions. Where the church is content to serve as the custodian of cultural values, the people of the community may seem outwardly pleased, but inwardly they cannot have respect for an institution which in practice betrays its profession to have a word from God which is to be the plumb line for personal, social, economic, and national life. Unless the church is led to a new exodus from its cultural captivity, it will not be able to fulfill its clear evangelistic mission with power and authenticity.

At the end of the Second World War, American judges and legal experts participated in the protracted months of the Nuremberg war trials. High-ranking officers of the German army as well as high-ranking civilian officials of the Third Reich faced trial for general acts which had violated the Geneva Articles of War and, more deeply, had violated the human conscience. World opinion was brought to bear against those who, like Adolf Eichmann, explained their actions as "only following orders given by superiors." Now, with the release of confidential and classified papers referred to as "The Pentagon Papers," together with a revelation of the torturous role of America in Vietnam, the American public has been engaged in a debate between conscience and national policies. It is apparent that evil comes about not only when people violate what they understand to be their duty, but evil may also be the result of what people do when they conscientiously fulfill what is expected of them. When the issue touched the German officials, the American conscience and the judgment of the church seemed very clear. But when matters are closer to home, as in the Calley court-martial, Americans are faced with the perplexing dilemmas of the role and function of the Christian conscience when it comes into collision with a national goal and its resultant duty. If, in peacetime, a church has difficulty in following the Christian gospel with its notes of transcendent judgment and grace, in wartime the task seems almost impossible.

Shortly after the outbreak of the First World War, it is said that H. G. Wells spent a succession of days during those first shattering weeks meditating among the tombs of a village churchyard. He kept recalling that in every town and village throughout the British Isles there were similar churches dedicated to the same Christian purposes. He wondered to himself quite often why he did not hear from the Christian pulpits, represented in this mighty and mysterious institution, some significant word of light and leading for the nations of the world. But where silence did not reign as quiet as the cemetery, the voices that he did hear were only the echoes of the nation and its national ideals and goals. [4] What Mr. Wells was intuitively feeling for and reflecting was that a national church is a denial of its faith. W. E. Orchard says that men in the world come to understand that underneath all of our Christian creeds and systems, which may appear on the surface to be different, the churches are very much alike because they are just like the world. He illustrates his point by referring to the nonconforming churches of England, who, under the pressure of the war spirit, surrendered their independence of conscience to assume the same national stance and to espouse the same doctrine as the established Church of England itself. He points out that first, the nonconforming churches surrendered their historic conscience by accepting a system of military conscription. On the heels of that, they let conscience be further violated as the state penalized those who resisted the war system on conscientious grounds. Orchard draws the biting conclusion that "For the sake of conscience a man may split the Church, but he must not split the nation."[5] In line with this cultural captivity of the contemporary church, W. H. Auden writes of his "Unknown Citizen," which also could stand as a parody upon the manner in which the church has been conformed by its culture rather than by transforming it by the renewing mind of Christ.

> Our researchers into Public Opinion are content
> That he held the proper opinions for that time of year;

When there was peace, he was for peace; when there was war, he went.
He was married and added five children to the population,
Which our Eugenist says was the right number for a parent of his generation,
And our teachers report that he never interfered with their education.
Was he free? Was he happy? The question is absurd:
Had anything been wrong, we should certainly have heard.[6]

The Christian gospel reveals God in the face of Jesus Christ, who, despite his birth in Palestine under Roman occupation, was both un-Jewish and un-Roman. He remains un-Russian, un-Chinese, un-American. Thus we should not be surprised to feel the backlash of pressure outside the church designed to restrict its freedom to be a critic of culture. If left alone, the transforming message of the Christian gospel would turn the world upside down today just as it did in areas of the first century in the Roman Empire. The force of both the state and cultural traditions are used as engines of intimidation as during Hitler's regime. Universities were purged; editors were silenced; books were burned; and, as the late Albert Einstein noted, one by one these free institutions lapsed into conformity with the Nazi ideology and tyranny. In too few places did the church in Germany stand out because its people fulfilled their roles as servants of the most High God, which restricted them from being vassals of the state and reflections of its inhuman and anti-Jewish cultural values. In the same way, in Russia, the state offers a form of religious liberty to the church. Preachers are given a freedom of the pulpit to say prayers and to lead in the singing of hymns if the church does not meddle in the affairs of state and nation. In Yugoslavia, religious liberty means "containment of the church." Religion is privatized. The public sector is off limits.

In America, we hear influential voices raised from time to time seeking to restrict the life of the church to its inward aspects only. The applause and support given to this thesis come not from Russia or Yugoslavia, but from citizens in high places and church members in free America. Church members themselves expect the pulpit to reflect the views of the congregation, and the views of the congregation are expected to reflect the views of the nation and its prevailing culture. Shrinking pledges, withheld financial and moral support, lagging budgets and attendance, and official action and sanctions make very visible the dissatisfaction of church members with a Christian message which rubs too hard against the grain of the established order of things. If the forces outside the church want a parrot and not a preacher, it is apparent that there are forces inside the church who want a puppet and not a prophet. Some good church people do not want the man of God to be like Moby Dick's preacher who, having climbed up into his pulpit in the form of a ship's prow by means of a rope ladder, pulled the ladder up after him, as if to signify thereby that there are no strings attached. But if the minister of Christ and the members of the congregation are not free together to think unthinkable thoughts, to entertain intolerable ideas, to speak unpalatable things, or to espouse unpopular causes, we can be sure that the church remains in cultural captivity to its national ideals and goals and requires a new exodus from Rome, the symbol of imperial sovereignty and nationalism.

In cultural captivity, the role of the church will be defined as custodial and clerical. But, after her exodus, the role of the church is to be a critic. The church as the critic faces a dilemma much like that of the dramatist who must decide whether he is going to attempt to please his audience or to present life as he feels it really is. Eric Bentley summarizes the issue by saying, "the playwright is either a rebel and an artist or a yes man and a hack." [7] The church always must be ready to play the role of the rebel who leads the struggle against entrenched evil and injustice in the status quo. If the church fails to fulfill this responsibility, then it becomes a "yes man" to its culture.

Whenever the church remains in its abject cultural bondage and is content to function as a national institution, it must define itself in ways that do not reflect faithfulness to the gospel. We are not surprised therefore to read how such a church turns away a black student and the chief usher says, in justifying that action, "This is a *private* institution." In contrast, one is reminded of Martin Luther King when he said:

> I would like to say to you that there are some things within our social system of which I am proud to be maladjusted. . . . I never intend to become adjusted to the

evils of segregation and discrimination . . . to adjust myself to economic conditions that will take necessities from the many to give luxuries to the few . . . to adjust myself to the madness of militarism and the self-defeating effects of physical violence.

In tracing the lives of prophets through the centuries who were maladjusted to some local malady, Dr. King concluded, "I am convinced that the world is in desperate need of such maladjustments." [8] In his book *The Bent World*, J. V. Langmead Casserley sounds a similar note when he confesses: ". . . in a fallen world the very fact that I am a conforming member of the Christian Church forbids me to be an out-and-out, unquestioning conformist in any other sphere of existence." In politics, in prevailing social mores, in the climate of social opinion, in all of his secular allegiances, Casserley concludes, ". . . under the authority and judgment of God. . . . It is my conformity that makes me a nonconformist." [9]

Lacking that conviction, the church in its evangelistic activities may be inviting unsaved people to accept an American Jesus or a denominational Jesus or a middle-class Jesus or some other Jesus. If we do, he will be but a pale fiction of the Christ of God, whom we meet as the Christ of faith in Jesus of Nazareth. What can evangelism mean to a church which is blind to the fact that it is not inviting its professed Christian members to think Christianly but to think conventionally? Must we not hear the word of Jesus as it came to Simon Peter in the sixteenth chapter of Matthew: "Get out of my way, you devil, your outlook is not God's outlook, but man's!" (Cf. Matthew 16:23.) Short of God's deliverance and our exodus, evangelistic activities of our local congregations and our denominations may turn out to be much like the man who had the task of blowing the noon whistle at the factory where he worked. Taking his responsibility seriously, he made it a point to check his watch every morning with the most accurate chronometer in a certain jeweler's window. One day out of curiosity he stepped inside the jewelry store and asked the owner if his chronometer was set by Western Union, Arlington Time Signal, or Naval Observatory Time. Surprised at the question, the jeweler replied that he did not use any of these sources; he simply set his chronometer by the factory whistle that blew every day at noon! If the church is to be more than an echo, reflecting its cultural conformity, it must experience a new exodus from its cultural captivity.

One need not underestimate the courage and heart which may be required in the task of challenging and correcting the bias and prejudice of any given age while calling into question the parochial loyalties and the nationalisms of a given period of human history. When Stalin was on his deathbed, it is said that he called Khrushchev to his side and told him, "I have prepared two letters. When you are in difficulty because of your economic policies and your five-year plans which have not worked out, open the first letter. Then, when you are in real trouble, and your very life itself is in danger, open the second letter." Later, after Stalin's death, when Khrushchev was in power and he was faced with a severe economic crisis, he remembered Stalin's advice and opened the first letter. It said simply, "Blame everything on me!" Khrushchev promptly unmasked Stalin as the source of all the Soviet woes. Then, several years later, in 1964, when the real showdown came in the Kremlin power struggle and Khrushchev's life was in dire danger, he feverishly opened the second letter. It said, "Prepare two letters!" One does not challenge domestic dreams, denominational bigotries, local idolatries, and cultural majorities, without facing the threat of those who, in open intimidation or in more quiet ways, say in effect to the minister of Jesus Christ and to the church of Christ, "Prepare two letters!"

The effectiveness of the church in its evangelistic mission will always be related to its integrity of life and faithfulness to the living God, who refuses to be boxed in by our national narrowness, our religious traditions, or our cultural conformity. Often he appears in unexpected places like Nazareth, in untraditional teachings like those of Jesus, in minority opinions like those of Caleb and Joshua, two of the spies sent out by Moses; or Roger Williams, founder of Rhode Island. His Presence with us and his Word within us, like a fire in our bones, will enable the church to face the hostility of its age and to say as did Joan of Arc:

Do not think you can frighten me by telling me that I am alone . . . it is better to be alone with God; His friendship will not fail me, nor His counsel, nor His love. . . . You will all be glad to see me burnt; but if I go through the fire I shall go through it to their hearts for ever and ever. And so, God be with me! [10]

Such a note of transcendence enables a reformer to say: "My conscience is captive to the Word of God; I cannot and I will not recant anything. For to go against conscience is neither right nor safe, God help me. Amen." Such a transcendent word of Christian witness manifest in our new exodus can regain the attention of a generation which has lost respect for the church except as it gives a tip of the hat as to an aged gentleman, who has outlived his usefulness but still manifests some marks of his humanity.

The impotence of the church issues from the irrelevance of the church. The irrelevance of the church is related to our asking people to give their lives to only half a Christ. But the New Testament affirms, "It is no weak Christ we have to do with, but a Christ of power." (Cf. 2 Corinthians 13:3.) If the church will not make room for its prophets who can lead her out of her cultural bondage, she will know in time only those priests who will exist to read the burial service for that imitation of God's faithful church.

W. A. Visser 'T Hooft warns us that such an alliance of the church with any one particular culture may seal its death and doom. He reminds us that the church in Carthage enjoyed all of the advantages of strength and power and intellectual acumen. It had been the church of Tertullian; it had been the church of Cyprian; it had been the church of St. Augustine. But the fact remained that the church did not live long after Augustine's death. It was the church of the Romans, and because it was never open to any un-Roman activities, it died.[11] On the opposite side, one of the astonishments in history is provided by the evident power of the radical self-criticism which we see in the life of Israel who, as the people of God, derive their strength from loyalties greater than nationalism and from moral values and spiritual insight which transcend their local settings. When the church's message and its evangelistic invitation yield to the temptation to make its words the echoes of the mass opinions everywhere entertained, we may succeed in getting people to join our churches, to be baptized, and to make their pledges, but we cannot believe that we are successful in our mission to introduce persons to Jesus Christ as Lord and Savior. Like Thoreau's "Distant Drummer," God's evangelist must keep step to the music which he hears, however distant or faraway. What matter if the world asks indignantly in the words of Job 18:4 (Moffatt), "Are things to be upset, because of you?"

7
An Exodus from Sinai

A lay church leader from Nebraska tells of a camping trip which her family, together with her parents, were enjoying. There were several vehicles and campers in the traveling party, and members of the family from time to time rode in different vehicles with a different group among the party. As a practical measure, they took a head count each time they stopped, lest they might leave someone behind. At one point, they made a comfort stop and got started again without counting noses. About thirty-five miles later, to their consternation, they discovered that their eight-year-old boy was missing. Quickly they turned around and drove back to the gasoline station where they had stopped earlier. They found their eight-year-old son inside, calmly reading a picture book, but his question was, "What took you so long?" [1]

Few people would deny that there are millions of human beings living in our world who are lost and forgotten, even as that boy. In Jesus' parable of the two sons (Luke 15), the older son is lost without ever having left home. Alienated from his father, he refuses to be reconciled to his brother. The younger son was alienated from himself and could not "come to himself" until he made up his mind to go to his father. Knowing the need of the human heart and its desperate homesickness for the living God, the church has an incredible piece of Good News to share with the world. As a personal Savior from sin, Jesus Christ offers forgiveness, a sense of glad release from the controlling power of the past, and the hope of a new beginning and of a new life which can be described like "being born again" or participating in "a new creation."

Although the church has this evangel, we find the church faithless and reluctant in pursuing its evangelistic mission. The world asks us in the words of the eight-year-old boy, "What took you so long?" How can we explain the loss of our sense of mission and the lack of urgency which characterize so much of our contemporary church life? When the Advisory Commission dealt with the theme "Christ—The Hope of the World" in preparation for the World Council of Churches Assembly in Evanston, it said, in part:

> The urgency of the Church's mission derives from the fact that its mission is the result of participation in the work of God. We can avoid the task of preaching the Gospel only by refusing to allow the Gospel to take possession of our lives. . . . It is because we have failed so largely to let the Gospel take possession of us that we have failed also so greatly to fulfil our evangelistic task. There is no other way of believing in the Gospel than by witnessing to it. If we really took our stand upon it we should be compelled by that very situation to be urgent in staking Christ's claim for all men and for all of life. If we but truly believed that Christ had already claimed the Hindus, the Buddhists, the Muslims, the Jews, the Communists, and the great pagan masses of our time for Himself, we should no longer skirt around these groups as hesitantly as we often do. Our evangelism is not to be determined by the likelihood of immediate response. It is to be determined by the nature of the Gospel itself.[2]

Beyond that general explanation, we have been saying, also, that the church's failure to find freedom, flexibility, and obedience for its evangelistic task is because of its crippling captivity. Missing the fellowship of the risen Christ on the Emmaus road, we are kept in our Egyptian captivity, in bondage to Athens, in bondage to Nicea, in bondage to Jerusalem, and in bondage to Rome. Our unexamined assumptions keep us from seeing our mission clearly; our captivity to unreformed creeds and to outworn words, our captivity to stereotyped methods, inflexible structures, and our captivity to cultural conformities and social conventions have limited our freedom and militated against a sense of urgency in fulfilling the Great Commission which Christ entrusted to his church. But, in addition, there are too few of God's people who are following Jesus in their daily life "to seek and to save that which is lost." This lack of faithfulness may be explained further because of our captivity in Sinai which symbolizes the dependence of the church upon a special set of religious symbols with a restricted altar and a special priesthood. Our captivity to clericalism perpetuates the patterns and stipulations received at Sinai which established the Levitical priesthood as a special and restricted ministry which made religion a monopoly in which no other member of the nation could share under pains and penalty of death. If the church is going to succeed in reducing the lead time presently required between hearing men from Macedonia call us to come and help them and our actual going, we need a new exodus from Sinai and its crippling, clerical captivity. An exodus from Sinai will result in our deliverance from a special to a universal priesthood. It will provide freedom from a monological to a dialogical style of Christian witness and leadership. It will lead us from the restricted precincts of a special religious class into the whole life of the world and the probing issues of our time which emerge out of man's relationship to God and to his neighbor.

In receiving the law, Moses instituted a restricted altar and a system of special sacrifices to be administered by a special priesthood. The Levites were to be a tribe set apart for the special service of the sanctuary and for the care of the sacred things (Numbers 1:44-54; 18:2; Deuteronomy 10:8; 18:5 ff.). The tribe of

Levi was to have no possessions, because the Lord, himself, was to be its inheritance (Deuteronomy 10:9; 18:2). The special priesthood was to have no business or worldly distractions which might take away or detract from their service of the house (Numbers 16:9). Sinai depicted the need for a special priesthood with special calling related to a holy place and to the care of holy things. No other member of the nation could participate in this holy service, under penalty of death (Numbers 3:10). In keeping with this concept, when the tribes of Israel were numbered to measure their military strength, the tribe of Levi was granted exception from anticipated military duty (Numbers 1:49-50).

Someone has quoted a contemporary who, in a moment of pique, declared that every profession seemed to be a conspiracy against the laymen. In law, lawyers keep the laymen dependent upon them by embalming the decrees of the court in "legalise"; in medicine, doctors keep laymen dependent upon them with their prescriptions written in an illegible Latin; in other branches of knowledge, scientists and mathematicians keep laymen dependent upon them by using mysterious symbols and signs that only the professional can decode and understand. So, with a special priesthood, the church hides its good news in a religious jargon and limits its evangelistic mission to a tribe of Levi.

But, if the Law was given by Moses and included a religious monopoly, grace and truth came by Jesus Christ and the ministry of the New Covenant passed from his hands, as Great High Priest, to become a universal rather than a local or special priesthood. It is said that, at the death of Jesus upon the cross, the veil in the temple in Jerusalem was rent in twain. New Testament writers assign a special significance to the symbolism of that fact. The veil was the heavy curtain between the Holy of Holies and the outer court in the temple and was designed to keep men out from the Holy Place except for the person of the great high priest who entered on the day of Atonement to offer sacrifice for the sins of the people. The writer of Hebrews says that the rending of the veil signifies that the world now has an accessibility to God in Jesus Christ which brings God within reach of every man by faith (cf. Hebrews 10:19-22). From the restricted priesthood of a single tribe, defined in the Sinai legislative code, we move into the ministry of the New Covenant where the grace of God has appeared in Jesus Christ qualifying all of God's people to enter into his continuing ministry. From Levi in the Old Testament to Levi the publican in the New Testament seems to involve us in an unlikely leap. Who seems to be less qualified than Levi, the despised tax collector, the publican? Yet, it is the call of Christ given to such men which convinces us that if grace is able to accept him so that he is eligible for the universal priesthood, other men like him, who might feel disqualified, can now have hope.

George Adam Smith interprets an interesting incident recorded in Second Chronicles (26:17) whereby an unauthorized person sought to usurp the rights of the Levitical priesthood and suffered a grievous penalty. Smith said had this man lived but a few centuries later, rather than being penalized for his affrontry, he would have been celebrated as the first Protestant! [3] We believe, indeed, that the church is not made up of a clerical class, but it is made up of the whole people of God. The church is not made up of first-class citizens known as the clergy and second-class citizens known as the laity. Quakers are misunderstood when it is said of them that they have no ministers. It might be said with as much accuracy that they have no laypeople. Every member is to be a minister.

In the life of the early church, we see the emphasis develop on a mutual participation and ministry which came in time to be described as the priesthood of all believers. The people, seeing the boldness of Peter and John, and perceiving that they were, in the words of the King James Version, "unlearned and ignorant men, they marveled; and they took knowledge of them, that they had been with Jesus" (Acts 4:13). The words in the original record, which have been unfortunately translated in the King James Version, included *idiotai* and *agrammatoi*. The first word, from which our English word for *idiom* is derived, signifies a private person or an amateur or layman. The second word speaks of one who has not had the benefit of a formal training at the feet of a Gamaliel, an Hillel, or other accepted doctors of the law. *Agrammatoi* means more than being "ungrammatical." It was obvious that the apostles were not members of a prophetic guild, nor had they had the benefit of the formal Jewish systems of endorsement and accreditation as religious teachers. Despite this, they were manifesting *parresia*, which was the term used to describe the freedom of speech available to the Greek citizen in the city-state. They were outsiders; yet they were using the language and participating as if they really did belong. The church was based in its life and ministry on a new reality of a universal priesthood which moved from Levi in the Old Testament to Levi the publican in the New.

However, exodus from our clerical captivity in Sinai includes also an exodus from a monological style of witness in which laypeople are to receive the right answers over many loudspeakers where there is but one microphone. Sometime ago I read an article by a theological professor who said, "To simplify is to falsify." At first glance, one is tempted to be put off by his assertion. His statement seems too much like a license for obtuse and abstract thought which finds expression in technical language and obscure jargon. But then we realize in making his simple point, he proved it. "To simplify is to falsify." But what was he getting at? He was pointing out that every simple statement of "a simple gospel" must leave out far more of the gospel than it is able to include. In effect, he was reminding us that the gospel came first of all in the event of Christ and not in a special religious vocabulary. The mutual ministry of a universal priesthood witnesses both to the objective event in Christ's total life story as well as to our personal experience and understanding of it. Laypeople are qualified to participate in the universal priesthood of Christian evangelistic witness because they are able to testify to what they have seen, handled, and tasted of the Word of life.

In his essay "On Slogans," Lenin tells us that the masses must be mobilized. The best way to do so is to rally them with simple formulas, giving them a "line" in the form of prefabricated responses which can fit any problem. These slogans could provide self-contained explanations of events which have enough truth in them to be plausible, but which spare people the pain of thinking and valuing which are the essential ingredients for every meaningful personal choice. Someone has described the man with a simple slogan as an ideologist running down the street shouting, "I've got an answer. Who has a question?" Slogans are like slot machines which promise us a big take for our nickle. In the end, they turn out to be one-armed bandits and we discover that "to simplify is to falsify."

In its evangelistic task today, the church faces the sobering questions, "Can we afford to learn from Lenin?" "Can we afford to embrace his methods?" In our desire to win others to Christ, we must be loyal to Jesus' methods as well as to his message. In his temptation, Jesus refused popular methods which had more the ring of a circus in them than the pain of a cross. He would not jump from the pinnacle of the temple as a religious showman saying, "Look at me!" He would not use bread to buy the loyalty of a fickle crowd; he would not yield to the temptation of surrendering the patience of God's kingdom for some shortcut to success. He would not falsify the fullness of God's truth by prepackaging the gospel in simple slogans which could be easily dispensed in memorized monologues. Jesus' method is quite the opposite from the ideologist who comes running, shouting, "I've got an answer! Who has a question?" Instead, Jesus is open and available to every person to help him see what it is in his life that keeps him trusting himself to God's love. Frequently our questions may actually camouflage or cloak the real problem which blocks our coming to Christ.

The difference between a monological and a dialogical style in ministry is reflected by Reuel Howe. He defines a dialogical person as *"a total, authentic person"* who is really present in the situation with a willingness to learn as well as to teach. Second, he identifies a dialogical person as one who is "open" with a willingness and an ability to reveal himself to others and an openness to hear and receive the revelation of others. He is both willing to be found out and he is willing to accept the response of others, whatever it is, as an important part for the whole learning process. Third, Howe indicates that a dialogical person is a disciplined person able to assume responsibility for himself and for others, giving himself freely and yet leaving freedom for the other person to respond as he will. Last of all, he indicates that a dialogical style demands a person who is related to other persons.[4]

In stressing this aspect of our mutual ministry and in refusing to accept the monological style of Lenin's propagandist and indoctrinator, there is a danger. Many Christians and lay leaders may think that they are getting a written excuse for their indolence, faithlessness, and silence. If the gospel cannot be "put up" in a simple package, who of us can be wise enough to understand it or can be qualified to witness so that others can be led to Christ? The gospel does speak of the unsearchable riches of Christ. The Bible does ask, "Who has fathomed the mind of God?" But despite the wealth which we have not yet fully discovered, despite the fact that we "know only in part," God does not excuse us from being one of his witnesses. Christ, himself, is God's evangel. The Holy Spirit is the evangelist. Our task is to witness to those places where Christ has vitally touched our lives. Because the Spirit of God is the evangelist, we can lose our anxiety about whether our "words" are going to win anyone else. Jesus, himself, was the Master Teacher. He came as God's most effective witness, but, according to the record, he did not win everyone he talked to. He would not manipulate men, nor would he manage their motives with coercive means or methods. In carrying on his work as a part of his universal priesthood, ministers and lay persons alike must be faithful to both his message and his methods.

In this connection there is a story about an inquisitive passenger on the rear platform of a long train, slowly winding its way along a broad French river. He was puzzled by the signs which they passed. He knew they were not mileposts because they were always the same series—100—125—150. He concluded that they could not be speed-limit signs because, with those sharp curves, no engineer could be making a hundred miles an hour and keep the train on the track. Finally he asked a flagman, "What do those signs mean?" The flagman answered, "Car lengths. There are so many car lengths to the switch. If it is a long train, the engineer can't see all of it at once around these long curves. But he knows how many cars he has got in his train, and the signs tell him whether or not the last car is out of the siding. You see," the flagman concluded, "the engineer's got to know where his hind end is."

An engineer does need to know where his hind end is, because if he does not know, he may think that the whole train is on the main line while some of it is still on the sidetrack. The engineer has a duty not only to look out ahead, but to think backward, and thinking backward means to think back all the way to the caboose. If the last car of his train is not past the siding, his train isn't past the siding. Likewise the teacher must know where the hind end of his class is. It is not enough merely to welcome the eagerness of the learners in the front row, but where are the students in the caboose? In the same way a minister must know where his congregation's hind end is; there may be some cars bumping along on the siding which have not yet reached the main track. He dare not go roaring down the main track, using the latest theological language while some boxcars back in the rear are still in high school and have never heard such language.

The only point I would change in this homely figure of speech is from viewing the minister as the engineer. All of the members on board belong to the crew and none can ride as passengers. We see Jesus' method with his disciples as the basis for the dialogical approach to the fulfillment of our Christian witness and evangelistic outreach. Jesus says, in effect, "I have many things to say to you, but they must wait." Line by line, bit by bit, he teaches us, patiently, lovingly, and lightly, until apprehension and comprehension begin to dawn upon us. If this is the Master's way with us, must we not see it as one of the most effective methods in the winning of others to follow him?

An exodus from Sinai and our captivity to clericalism would not only free the whole church to participate in the evangelistic outreach of the church, but will also free us from making our religious practices ends in themselves. We shall be helped to see that an exodus from Law to grace, from Moses to Christ, delivers us from a religion of external and legal means to a Christian experience of vital and personal proportions. We shall see that in Jesus Christ both the spiritual and the temporal meet together in his life and work. Unless we experience such an exodus, we will be unable to help those who regard the world and the church as not only separate, but as enemies. Those who hold this view see the world as a distraction to man's religious life, which is defined as custody and care of the temple by a special priesthood. The life of piety is thus understood as an inward relationship of private immediacy to God which has neither time nor room for horizontal relationships to either our neighbors or society.

In this view, the mission of the church is best understood by the role of the lifeguard at the ocean's edge who stands ready to throw out the lifeline and rescue the perishing from the alien and hostile surf. Our natural life is regarded as an enemy of our spiritual life, and our attitude and stance toward the world must be like the tribe of Levi, one of disengagement and separation. From this viewpoint, the religious life still involves sacred shrines and special symbols and holy seasons. The veil of the temple is accepted as a necessary barrier to keep bad men out and to shelter those inside who have found a haven and a refuge under the horns of the altar. The splitting of the veil by the event of Christ's cross must be regarded as the desecration of the temple rather than the consecration of the whole of man's historical existence. If the church is serving as the tribe of Levi, the life of the world must remain as a distant threat to be held in check by a moat across which the voice of the special priesthood in the church is to be raised periodically in a watchman's warning. When the Christian witness is confused with memorized propositional statements which are to be declared, those who have the best memories turn out to be the best Christians or witnesses; so when the church is disengaged from the life of the world, those who have the strongest voices, which can carry the deepest into the camp of the hostile enemy, have the best chance for success. This style of Christian witness, borrowed from the tribe of Levi, yields the practical result that we are as successfully separated and insulated from the questions of our day and from the men of our day as if we had taken holy orders in a medieval monastery. We miss the meaning of Jesus' command when he breathed upon his disciples and said, "As my Father has sent me forth into the world, even so send I you" (cf. John 17:18; 20:21).

We must come to see that the rending of the veil in the temple at the time of the crucifixion of Jesus signified the end of a religious monopoly where God was accessible only to a special priesthood. The broken veil does not mean the temple of God has been desecrated or that the sabbath has been profaned. Instead, it signifies that God is acting in the life of the world to consecrate man's whole life so that each day a person may offer himself as a living sacrifice to God. The rent veil signifies the end of clericalism with a special, exclusive priesthood. Now the whole people of God are to be involved in the mutual ministry of Christian faith, witness, and service. The priesthood of all believers means the end of a double standard. Just as Levi was to minister in the life of the Tabernacle, so now the members of God's body are to serve the life of the world, so that out of a holy fellowship of love, persons may be led to trust themselves in personal commitment to Jesus Christ as Lord and Savior.

Someone has told the story of an American couple who were touring one of the great teeming cities of the world. Looking out from the car in which they were traveling together with a guide, the husband saw an object of merchandise that he thought his wife might like. Instructing the driver to stop, he jumped out of the car to the side of the bazaar and began to haggle about the price. The poor people of the city, noting him to be an American, began to press in upon him, begging for money. Pushing and shoving, they sought to get to him with their hands outstretched. The guide in the car felt perhaps that the man's life or possessions might be in danger. Quickly, he jumped out of the car and pushed his way through the unruly mob, grabbed the American, and shoved him back into the car. Meanwhile, the crowd had become angry because they saw themselves losing the opportunity to get even a single coin. They surged toward the car, and as the guide jumped in after the American, the car began to pull off almost before the doors were closed. But then suddenly, out of the crowd, a man, holding a terribly emaciated, scrawny baby in his arms, pushed the baby through the front window of the car into the lap of the astonished American woman. As he did so, he said, in broken English, "Your baby, your baby!" In that circumstance the guide reached over and grabbed the baby from the lap of the American woman, and he pushed it back through the car window into the arms of the father, as the car sped away. But, in a more profound sense, God has thrust the whole world into our hands. We know that God has so loved the world that he gave his own Son for its salvation. Christians are people to whom God has given that selfsame world to love and to serve.

In a penetrating interpretation of Dostoevsky, Roger Cox underscores this sense of responsibility to the world, which, though unlovable, requires our presence and our sacrifice. He writes:

> If we refuse to love those things which are not lovable, we lose the capacity to love those which are. . . . By the same token, if we reject responsibility for those things which are not specifically our fault, we cannot properly assume responsibility for those which are. This happens because when we disclaim, in retrospect, all responsibility for evils and suffering which we did not actually cause, we create, in prospect, evils and sufferings for which we *are* to blame.[5]

In thinking about our evangelistic mission to the world and to each person in it, the whole church must go for all because someone has gone for us! By his amazing grace, God is waiting to deliver us from our bondage in Sinai and to lead the whole church in a new exodus wherein every Christian serves as an evangelist.

8
An Exodus from Babylon to Bethlehem

The theme of this chapter reflects a simple thesis. When Israel was in bondage to Egypt and in exile in Babylon, the only world open to her was the private world of religion. The people of God had no responsibility for political decisions. They had neither lot nor part with the Egyptians or the Babylonians in the public decisions which were made in those nations. After a Pharaoh who arose and knew not Joseph, and after the people of Israel had become slaves, and later as captives in Babylon, they had no vote, no way to influence the political decisions of the government directly. We make a profound mistake when we assume the possibilities of our twentieth-century democratic franchise in our

consideration of life under world powers which were more totalitarian and autocratic. Thus, as slaves and exiles, Israel had no
access to the agencies which dictated the social policies of the
state. The conditions of their daily life allowed them only to fulfill the demands of their servitude and their captivity. They were
free to make bricks with or without straw, depending upon
the whims of the Pharaohs, the kings, and their straw bosses. As a
captive people in Babylon, they exercised no political franchise.
They were allowed to maintain identity as a separate people, but
they had no measurable involvement in helping to run the
affairs of state and nation.

When they were asked to sing a song in Babylon, the psalmist
asked plaintively, "How shall we sing the Lord's song in a foreign
land?" (Psalm 137:4). Babylon was not their real home. They lived,
prayed, and hoped for the day when the Lord's hand would deliver
them out of the house of bondage and the land of their exile.
Meanwhile, the life that seemed most open to them was the life of
religion in its private and interior aspects. If they did not possess
freedom to use political power as an engine of persuasion or force,
they were able to experience an inward freedom. But as Israelites,
they did not have the opportunity to share responsibility in
making Babylonian history or in shaping national institutions.

However, we would be guilty of denying history and of
misunderstanding the Old Testament if we did not concede that
the persistent faith and inward history of the people of God, in
bondage and in exile, was not without a profound effect upon the
affairs of state and nations, both in Egypt and in Babylon. Indeed,
there are notable occasions when the inward faith of individuals
promoted them to great positions of honor and prominence in the
new land. One cannot forget Queen Esther, Nehemiah, or Daniel.
One cannot ignore the presence of Joseph as prime minister of
Egypt in an earlier day; but we see these persons as notable exceptions who do not represent the common lot of the people of God in
Egypt or in Babylon.

Our thesis, therefore, is that the church of Jesus Christ, with
some exceptions, has mistakenly embraced a style of life and mission based on the pattern of the life of Israel in Egyptian bondage

and in Babylonian captivity. In America, in a real sense, we got what we asked for—we disestablished the church, saying that we didn't want a national church; and we do not have one. But the wall of separation between state and church has often been so high and so misunderstood that it has committed the church to a life of disengagement and to a style and pattern like Israel's life in bondage and in exile. One practical result of this disengagement from American history has been to allow a civil religion to develop apart from the Christian faith itself. This well-established civil religion functions with its own creed (the Declaration of Independence and the Bill of Rights of the United States Constitution). It has also its own holy days (Independence Day, Thanksgiving Day, Memorial Day), its own sacred men like the martyred presidents, its own unifying symbol in the flag, which is invested heavily with religious, inward emotion.[1]

This style of historical absenteeism and disengagement is better understood when we see the strands of thought in the Bible which are interpreted to describe Babylon as the adversary of God's people. Babylon, the harlot, stands over against Jerusalem, the golden. In addition, there are certain biblical texts which, if understood in a certain way, not only appear to justify the church's Babylonian style of life, but also would seem to commend that style of life on the part of all who would live in uncompromising fidelity to God. "Come out from them, and be separate from them" (2 Corinthians 6:17) is one appeal often quoted as justification for the separation of the church from the world and its awful evil. "Do not love the world" (1 John 2:15*a*) is another text which seems to support the contention that this is an evil world to which the devoted Christians are to give neither their hearts nor their time nor their presence. Many additional verses from the Bible could be used to support the style of life which, at best, encourages a neutrality on the part of the church in the land where it lives and, at the worst, an actual withdrawal from the life of the world. This theme occurs in many guises—the world is evil; its life is to be shunned; the church and its members are good and can remain good only by being "spiritually" occupied; the secular world is off limits; only by withdrawing from the world into the safety and the sheltered sanctuary of the church, can one find salvation and peace.

If one accepts this point of view, he must overlook many other texts of the Bible or spiritualize them and thereby empty them of their full impact. In the familiar words of John 3:16, "God so loved the world," "world" is often interpreted to mean either the good people in the world or the believing people in it. Second Corinthians 5:19, "God was in Christ reconciling the world to himself" can, by a quick exercise of rapid thought, be interpreted to mean the church. But we cannot escape the demand to reexamine our perspectives and our stance in the light of our knowledge that Jesus commanded his disciples to go into the world and to disciple the world. In Matthew 13:38, Jesus says plainly, "the field is the world." Because we have come to associate "the seed" with the gospel itself, we are startled to hear him as he continues: "the good seed means the sons of the kingdom!" What is his expectation but that the people of God are to be plowed and scattered in the furrows of the world? If we are to be the salt of the earth, Christians cannot remain separate in a container on the shelf. If we are to be the light of the world, Christians cannot let their light shine under a bushel. If we are to be the yeast, Christians must expect God to mix us with the dough which is to be leavened.

Part of the misunderstanding resides in the fact that often "the world" is confused with "the age." In the verse "The children of this age are wiser in their generation than the children of light" (Luke 16:8, author's paraphrase), the sons of the kingdom are contrasted with the sons of the age. This age passes away. This age with its structures, its demons, its powers above, and its powers below often stands in the way of God's kingdom. Christians are not to give themselves to the spirit of this age or to the demonic powers of the age. But Christians cannot follow Jesus Christ as his disciples without embracing God's love for the world and following him into the world. When Jesus promises to his disciples that the gates of hell shall not prevail against the church, we are often prone to misunderstand the symbolism of that text. We picture the church safely protected behind its ramparts and its walls, believing that the gates of hell shall not be able to destroy the church as it stands in magnificent isolation and retreat from attacking forces.

But to look at the text again is to recognize that the gates of hell represent the stationary aspects of the picture, and it is the church which is to be the moving, mobile force. The church can only attack; the gates of hell are on the defensive. Jesus assures us that the advance of the church cannot be stopped because even the gates of hell shall fall before her.

Thus, our theme asks us to see the necessity for the church to experience an exodus from Babylon and its historical absenteeism to Bethlehem, where, in the fullness of time, God sent forth his Son, born of a woman. The birth of Jesus, the New Testament plainly declares, was an historical event. It took place when Augustus was emperor of Rome, when Quirinius was governor of Syria, when Herod was king. Bethlehem stands for incarnation. The Word became flesh and dwelt among us and we beheld the glory of the Father and his only Son, full of grace and truth (cf. John 1:14). The incarnation settled the question as to whether matter is the seat of evil and the material structures of the world are to be shunned. In the beginning, the Bible declares, God made matter and called it good (cf. Genesis 1:31). God had fashioned the material structures of the world and had placed man in them and over them. In the incarnation, God once again took matter and used it as a vehicle whereby the life of Christ could come inside the life of the world. The incarnation and the subsequent ministry of Jesus settled the question as to whether God intended there to be an artificial boundary between the world and the church, between the secular and the spiritual. To be "spiritual," we understand now, does not mean to be invisible or immaterial. It is the insistence of the Bible, underscored in the incarnation, that everything which God has made is good (cf. 1 Timothy 4:4).

The incarnation settles the question of God's relationship to history and to time and the relationship which the people of God must have to history if they are to be faithful and obedient to God and his mission. If God would not leave the abyss of life alone, the church cannot afford to be undisturbed in its comfortable, historical absenteeism, which regards this world only as an anteroom where men are to wait until real life begins somewhere else. The Good News of the gospel teaches us that God has not left us as orphans in the world, but that we have a heavenly Father, that he is a God of history, where he is working out his purposes. We come then to understand and to confess that this is our Father's world, that the New Age is already here, even though hidden dimensions and future aspects of it are not yet realized by men. The God of the Bible, to whom the Scriptures bear witness and who calls his people to follow him, is One who does participate in the real life of the world. In history and in time God is at work to fulfill his original intent in creation and to restore what man in his perversity has marred, so that, once again, the material things of this world might serve and glorify their Maker.

The incarnation in the life of Jesus, with its demonstration of obedience to the Father, gives body and character to the atonement which Jesus made upon his cross and settles the question as to whether a wall still stands between God and man, between the races of men, between the religions of men, or between the reality of the church and the reality of the world. In Christ, the wall has been abolished and the enmities have been taken by him and nailed to his cross where he triumphed over them openly (cf. Ephesians 2:14-17; Colossians 2:13-15).

If the church has blundered and handicapped her evangelistic mission by adopting thoughtlessly or blindly the style of life and work suggested by Israel's life in its Egyptian bondage, or in its Babylonian captivity, the church can find remedy and relief for her mistake by an exodus from Babylon to Bethlehem, where she begins to participate in her responsible mission as the body of Christ, extending the work of his incarnation into the life of the world until the end of time. How can the church satisfy its claim to be the continuing body of Christ in the world if she abandons the Father's mission which brought Christ into the world at Bethlehem? As we trace Jesus' public ministry, we see him seldom at the center of religious occasions. But, amid the daily life of men, he is often found preaching and teaching, healing and helping, making God real to men, and bringing the touch of God's forgiving grace upon their lives. In the book of Acts, there is a note of discontinuity as the newly established church hesitates in fear in Jerusalem. But as it prays together and seeks to understand its new task, it begins to move in the same way as did its Master. We are led to understand that Jesus, no longer in the body of his incarnation, but Jesus, incarnate now in the life of his church, continues his work, not on many religious days or places or seasons, but in the midst of the life of men, bringing God close through grace and the gospel.

Our thesis is a simple one, but it has profound implications. The exodus from Babylon to Bethlehem leads us from a life of separation and disengagement in Babylon to a life of involvement implicit in the incarnation of Jesus Christ. The incarnation—God manifest in the flesh—speaks of his continuing presence inside history. "My Father is working still, and I am working" (John 5:17), said Jesus. The book of Acts could be described as accurately as the Acts of the Risen Jesus, rather than the Acts of the Apostles, because it is his presence with the church through his Spirit which illumines, inspires, and empowers its life and work.

Moreover, the ascension of Jesus is misunderstood if we think of this event as celebrating the departure of Jesus from the life of the world. The significance of Olivet lies in its witness to the kingship of Jesus. He is exalted and given a name which is above every name. God has made him both Lord and Christ. In our evangelistic preaching, persons are often invited and urged to make Christ Lord of their lives. In our hymns, we are asked to "crown him king." In a real sense, persons do not make Christ Lord. He is already established by God's action as Lord of lords and King of kings. God did not hold an election to decide if he should send his Son to be the Savior of the world. Quite apart from man's decision or man's feelings, God acted to send his Son as the Savior of the world. Nor did God put it to a popular vote as to whether the false rulers of this world and the powers of darkness were to be deposed so that the rightful ruler could ascend his throne. The business of the church, in proclaiming its evangel, is to announce what has already taken place and to declare that God is the God of the whole earth and all its people, and He has the whole world in his hands and on his heart.

God's plan is to bring all creation together, everything in heaven and on earth with Christ as head (Ephesians 1:10). God's purpose

47572

has a much wider scope than the formation of a church as an organized institution; it includes the completion and fulfillment of his sovereign purpose based on what he had decided from the very beginning (Ephesians 1:11). So, Christ, himself, has reconciled mankind to God, breaking down the wall that kept men apart in order to create a single new people in union with himself (Ephesians 2:11-18). In this new union, every family in heaven and on earth receives its true name (Ephesians 3:15). The same notes of sweeping cosmic purpose and historical significance and involvement are sounded by the apostle Paul in Colossians. Through his Son, God acted to bring the whole universe back to himself, making peace through his Son's death upon the cross and so brought back to himself all things both on earth and in heaven (Colossians 1:19-20). In Romans 8:21 we hear of a hope that creation, itself, will one day be set free from its slavery and will share the glorious freedom of the children of God. God's intention has never been anti-historical; rather, immersed in the middle of history, he is acting not only to uphold the world by the Word of his power, but to sum up all things in Christ.

We would agree, therefore, with A. R. Vidler when he says,

> "The Bible, if you take it as a whole, leaves us in no doubt that God is interested in the welfare of nations and states as well as of the church; he is interested in legislation as well as in love, in hygiene as well as in holiness, in work as well as in worship, in art as well as in devotion, and it is to be presumed that where God is interested Christians should be so too." [2]

The exodus of the church from its exilic captivity, which separates it from the life of the world and the real history, is required by the truth of Bethlehem which speaks of God's real relationship with his world. He made the world, he loves the world, he sustains the world, he redeems the world, he reconciles the world, and he is at work in the world.

God has a relationship to his church and the people in it, as he seeks to give definite shape and structure and power for its life and mission. But it is no less his action when he calls us from our past securities and from the shelter of our established systems to move out into new forms and styles of mission. Like Abraham, to meet

God and to hear his call is to be open to the future of hope and to live a missionary, rather than a marginal historical existence. God also has and maintains a direct relationship to the world itself. His acts are not limited to the church and he does not fulfill his work only in professedly religious institutions. Indeed, the Bible is the record of how God acted in unexpected ways and places with unanticipated results. We find him in Ur of the Chaldees, calling a people to a covenant relationship. We watch God in Egypt, dealing with the Egyptian Pharaoh and the structures of political power there. We are as surprised as Jonah, to discover that God is in Nineveh, dealing not with men as individuals, but with the whole life of the city. For those who thought that God was shut up in the Holy Land, they were surprised to discover his presence with his people outside the religious boundaries of Israel. We see God at work in the life of Cyrus, a pagan king, whom he identifies as "his Messiah," the instrument of his purpose in history. Thus, God is acting in the church and through the church, but he is also acting outside the church and his actions are not limited to the church. His presence invests each aspect of his creation with meaning because of his ultimate purpose, which is to complete the body of Christ as the one, who, himself, completes all things everywhere, so that, in the end, "God may be everything to everyone" (1 Corinthians 15:28; see Ephesians 1:22; 1 Corinthians 15:24-28).

People have often misunderstood the urgent necessity of their evangelistic witness. They hear the word of Jesus when he says, "You shall be my witnesses in Jerusalem and in all Judea and Samaria and to the end of the earth" (Acts 1:8). They interpret this to mean that there are waiting cities and nations of the world in which the presence of God is absent until the first Christian appears. To reflect on the meaning of the missionary activity of God in the Old Testament and the missionary activity of Jesus revealed in the incarnation, we must believe that there is no place in the whole wide world where God's power and presence do not extend. God is already present by his Spirit in Jerusalem, in Judea, in Samaria, and in the faraway places of the world. And his Spirit is working inside the structures of history so that as the apostle Paul came to understand, God has not left himself without a witness, even if it is only the witness of creation, itself, which speaks about the majesty of God (cf. Acts 14:17; Romans 1:20).

Thus, when Philip was led to a lonely desert road, he discovered that God's Spirit preceded him and prepared the heart of a man of Ethiopia so that he was ready and receptive for the witness of Christian faith. While the apostles were still in Jerusalem, the news came that Samaria had received the Word of God. God was there before they got there. In another city, there was Lydia, a seller of purple, whose heart God had already touched and opened prior to the apostolic testimony. In another place, Cornelius, a Gentile, had heard God speaking about the realities of his kingdom.

Thus, the meaning of this text of Jesus is to assure us that the mission belongs to God and not to us. We enter it, we participate in it, but on the terms of him to whom the mission itself belongs. The evangelistic mission is always God's call to the church, to follow him where his Spirit already is at work preparing the hearts of individual men to accept Christ, and preparing the hearts and the lives of nations in history and in time to be the instruments of his purpose. Because God's mission in history includes reconciling action, it is necessary for us to follow him into the structures of history and into the personal relationships where alienation persists. Because I, as an individual, am alienated from the life of God in Christ, the Christian witness of the church must come to me to help me name my experience in the light of Christ's grace and lordship. Where there is alienation in the several communities of the world, the church has the responsibility to be an agent of reconciling action. When there is alienation in the life of the church itself, God intends the church to be present to herself to speak his word of reconciliation.

The church of Christ may be described in three technical terms. The church is an "empirical" organization. That means that the church itself shares the same uncertainties, risks, and contingencies of other organizations which are made up of human beings with their limited understandings, their partial knowledge, their fallible minds, and their uncertain futures. The church is not a pure organization made up of perfect people, but it discovers that its life is constantly shaped by its experience and by its own history.

One need not elaborate the life of weakness which the church has lived across the centuries.

But the church is also spoken of as "eschatological." This strange term means that the church participates in and lives by a power and a presence which transcends its limited history and its empirical existence. The church knows a divine presence and power and has access to the final resources which lie in God's grasp. To say that the church is an eschatological community is to define the church not in terms of what it is or what it has been, but in the light of what it is becoming. The powers of the new age, revealed in Jesus Christ, are at work in the life of the church. If the empirical existence of the church speaks of an institution that rises up out of the natural life of the world, to speak of the church as eschatological is to describe a community which reflects God's presence and power here and now as well as his ultimate purpose.

But the church must also be described as "ecumenical." This word is now used to describe interdenominational or interchurch relationships. Although this description does reflect the intent of given denominations to work in Christian mission mindful of the whole church of Christ, we need to understand that the word "ecumenical" had a much larger meaning in its original setting. In the New Testament, *oikoumene* referred to the whole inhabited earth and was not a religious term. The church is ecumenical only to the degree that it has been delivered from its exilic bondage in Babylon to its incarnational involvement in history symbolized by Christ's birth in Bethlehem. Thus, the church is ecumenical when it participates in the purposes of God and proclaims the Lordship of Christ over the whole earth and serves as a faithful witness of God's intent to renew the earth and to reconcile all things unto himself whether they be things in earth or things in heaven.

A theological professor once asked a class of young ministers what interested them most about the story of the good Samaritan, told by Jesus. He gained several replies dealing with aspects of the story. But one young man said, "What interests me most is the condition of the road between Jerusalem and Jericho." An ecumenical church is one which is following Christ in ministering to the victims who have been stripped, beaten, robbed, and left half-dead by the side of the road, and in telling them about the coming of a Savior into the world. But, also, an ecumenical church must work with fellow Christians and with other agencies in the world which may not yet be Christian, so that we can repair the condition of the road and make it safer for travelers who follow us. The evangelistic task of a church, therefore, is concerned about the salvation of individuals, one by one, but the church also shares the compassion and concern of Christ to combat the demonic forces which not only drive pigs over the cliff but also drive men out of their minds.

The incarnational style of Christian witness and ministry may require a new definition of spirituality. Two Scotsmen visiting together found themselves discussing the attributes of a new minister. One said, "Our new minister is the closest thing to deity that we've ever had in our kirk." His friend raised his eyebrows with a question, "How do you mean that?" "Well," his friend rejoined, "our new minister is invisible all through the week, and incomprehensible on Sunday." Often the church has defined what it means to be spiritual as being invisible and immaterial, unrelated to the structures and the history and the life of the world. Often, "spiritual" has come to mean the opposite of material, worldly, physical, or secular. Yet we would probably agree that Jesus was the most spiritual person who ever lived. But he constantly confused and bewildered people by his spirituality. Many of them thought that spirituality was fasting, and Jesus went to banquets. Some of them thought spirituality was seriousness, and Jesus perplexed them with his sense of humor, such as speaking of a camel going through the eye of a needle. Some thought that spirituality was separation from the pleasures of the world, and Jesus perplexed them by going to the wedding feast in Cana of Galilee and enjoying the presence and the company of other men. In the light of the way in which Jesus immersed himself in the joys and sorrows and the affairs of secular life, we draw the conclusion that the spiritual person is not one who abandons his body or the world to live as a withdrawn recluse or ascetic. The contemporary church is still afflicted with the views of gnosticism, which made matter the source and seat of evil and so could not really believe that the Word actually became flesh. The incarnation of Jesus not only gives us a new understanding about the dignity of our bodily existence as human beings, but also roots our lives as Christians in the life of the world, where we are to witness and serve.

John Oman reminds us

> The test of a true faith is the extent to which its religion is secular. . . .
>
> In the life of Jesus nothing is more conspicuous than His meagre interest in specially sacred doings, and His profound interest in the most ordinary doings of the secular life.[3]

In his parables Jesus seldom drew imagery from the special religious life of an especially religious time, but he took note of the procession of people in the midst of their secular occupations. C. H. Dodd makes a similar point when he observes, "Some religions lay such exclusive stress on the inward and spiritual, and therefore individual, aspect of religion, that the social and historical aspect falls away. Christianity has never been content with this." Pointing out that the Christian faith does not lag behind other religions in exalting the person's commerce with God in the "secret place of the Most High," Dodd observes that the Christian faith does not allow itself "to abide there undisturbed. It is concerned to make history." Being "an historical religion," Dodd concludes, it is "a social religion." [4]

The Hellenistic understanding of the religious world placed the gods in some distant Olympus where they were uninvolved and unrelated to the problems and precarious existence of the life of men. The Greek gods could care less about what happened to a man, as the inscrutable fates worked out the problems of human existence and the tragedies which befell man. In much the same way, the Oriental religions of mysticism look with despair on the reality of the world. Things and events are seen as a veil of illusion, concealing God from men. Only as the individual cuts himself loose from his social environment, forgetting time and entering eternity, through the negation of what to us makes life distinctively human, can a man be expected to penetrate to the mystery of God.

In the religions of mysticism we see, for example, outside every Buddhist shrine or temple the face of the Buddha—motionless, passionless, undisturbed, unconcerned, uninvolved with the squalor, the poverty, the disease, and the need of the people in that land. To the contrary, here and there one may see a Christian chapel, and on the chapel there may be the form of a cross. Which view of life is more akin to the heart of God? Is it the face of Buddha, untouched, unmoved, uninvolved in the affairs of men? Or is it the passion of Jesus Christ, who reflects the love of God, who is burdened with our human hurt, who feels the stab of our own heartache, who is bound up in human needs which prompted, at times, tears of concern? Yet the concern of Jesus, while being always personal, is also social. We cannot neglect the condition of the road. The Christian evangelist faces the constant temptation to define the Christian experience only in terms of inward piety and personal mysticism. This definition leads to a false dualism between spirit and matter, soul and body, sacred and secular, church and world, the things of God and the things of man. If this approach is followed, man's world, removed from the claim of Christ's Lordship, is allowed to veer in its own direction. Man's social, economic, and political spheres become more inhuman and unlivable as they are allowed to exist in a world apart from grace and the gospel. But what seems worse, is that the Christian life, divorced from the social settings of daily life, becomes a universe of religious formulas. A man is thought to be living a good Christian life when he knows the right words to say, rather than actually living in a right relationship to God and to his neighbors. An exodus from Babylon to Bethlehem will enable the church to discover that bringing men to Jesus as Lord and Savior does not bring them to a religion or an experience of escape, but of engagement.

But to believe in a real incarnation of God in Christ makes it imperative for us to affirm that God is inside the world he has made and which he has redeemed and reconciled in Christ. At the same time, he transcends and stands over against the world of nature, history, and of religion. To believe that God is only to be found inside the world of nature tends toward pantheism; to believe that God is only to be found outside the natural world tends toward a mechanical determinism and deism. Our Christian faith affirms that God, who stands over against us, also stands near us because he has come to us in Christ and remains accessible and available inside the structures of time and history. This world is more than a temporary stage upon which Christ appeared for a brief span of time. Not only does the world have a value and worth of its own as part of the creation of God, but the world and the nations which are in it occupy a part in the drama of history itself. The new people of God have a measurable identity because of the center around which they are constituted. But they have a circumference which is unmeasurable.

Some people are embarrassed by "the scandal of particularity": of Jesus of Nazareth, who was born in Bethlehem of the Virgin Mary, who suffered under Pontius Pilate, whose life and cross and resurrection took place as the founding events of the church. In their embarrassment, these people seem to deny the reality of the historical center. But others in the church are more often embarrassed by the limitless circumference of Jesus' life. Jesus seems able to include so many persons whom we want to shut out, because their difference is so threatening to our identity and our security. There was a woman of Samaria, who had her own arrangement of living in a commune; there was Zacchaeus, who appeared to have grown wealthy by dishonest fraud and deceit; there was Mary Magdalene; and there were other women of the street, too unrespectable for most of us! But the circumference of the circle which has Christ as its center is not rigidly fixed by man's scruples or fears. Just when we have drawn our circle and are finding it cozy and comfortable, we discover that God is extending the radius to require a larger circle. God's people cannot afford to lose the center which the church has in Jesus Christ, but neither can they act to limit the circumference of God's continuing mission which extends to the uttermost parts of the earth. God seeks to bring each person into a relationship of personal faith and commitment to Christ and to bring nations to walk in his ways, so that his will may be done on earth even as it is done in heaven.

When Rip Van Winkle dozed, he fell into a sleep which lasted for twenty years. When Rip fell asleep, there was a portrait over the fireplace in the inn. It was a picture of King George III, of England. Twenty years later, when he woke up, the painting of the

British king was gone. In its place, there was the visage of George Washington. Rip Van Winkle had slept through the period of the American Revolution! We confess that historical issues are often complexing, positions are easily polarized, and extremists are often vocal and militant. It is difficult for us as Christians to know where we should stand in these perplexing and revolutionary times. Obviously the safest place would seem to be for us to follow Rip Van Winkle into a long, quiet, peaceful sleep. We could hope that, upon awakening, we would discover that the vast, complex problems of our revolutionary world had been solved while we slept. We would thus be spared the pain of listening to the clamorous, confusing, and divided voices around us. We would be spared the pain of being confronted by our own sins and their social progeny and products. We would be spared the pain of personal repentance and commitment, of responsible decision, and of sacrificial involvement and engagement. But tempting as this solution might seem to us in the church in our weaker moments, we have to face the question as to what kind of world it would be twenty years from now, or ten years from now, if all Christians were suddenly to drop out of their society in sleep, leaving the decisions in community, city, state, nation, and world to those who have no Christian conscience, concern, compassion, or commitment to Jesus Christ! While the church cannot claim to have a Christian solution for every world problem and every local problem, the church must be prepared to be as vulnerable as Jesus was in his life and work. The church is not an infallible instrument so that we can always be sure that we are reading God's mind accurately or interpreting his will and purposes faithfully. In serving as his witness in the world, we run the risk of saying, "Lo, here is our God," when God is not at all involved in the cause which we have made our own, or he was involved for a different reason than that assigned to him so confidently by us.

As Christians, we cannot always be sure which party or which candidate or which nation may be used by God as the instrument of his purpose, as he used Cyrus and Caesar many centuries ago. But, as C. S. Lewis points out, that is not what Christianity guarantees.

When it tells you to feed the hungry it doesn't give you lessons in cookery. When i
tells you to read the Scriptures it doesn't give you lessons in Hebrew and Greek, o
even in English grammar. It was never intended to replace or supersede the
ordinary human arts and sciences: it is rather a director which will set them all to
the right jobs, and a source of energy which will give them all new life. . . . [5]

Lewis also points out that to expect the clergy alone to put on a
political program is asking for something impossible and for
which ministers may not have been trained. He illustrates his point
by assuring us that the presence of Christian people in business or
education or other vocations, as well as in politics, is the effective
means for the church to discharge its Christian responsibility,
helping to shape history in the light of faith and the gospel. He
goes on to say, "Christian literature comes from Christian
novelists and dramatists—not from the bench of Bishops getting
together and trying to write plays and novels in their spare time." [6]
What is really called for is a new dimension of faith in the priesthood of all believers and in the acceptance of daily work as a
vocation from God which offers the agenda for our service and
loyalty to Jesus Christ.

In his essays on church and state, Karl Barth tells us that if the
preaching of the whole gospel of the grace of God is to include the
whole of man's life, it must include political man and the
institutions which are shaped into society by political and social
action. Barth states: "This gospel which proclaims the King and
the Kingdom . . . is political from the very outset, and if it is
preached to real . . . men . . . it will necessarily be prophetically
political." Noting what an unhealthy condition it is when Christian people are frightened by "a political sermon," Barth asks if
preaching did not include such a dimension, how would it show
that it is the salt and the light of the world? [7] His profound
warning emerges from his experience with the temptation of the
German church to historical absenteeism during the life of Hitler.

We are warned that the church must not develop the habit of
arriving on the scene too late, when all the risks have been removed
and its presence doesn't really matter. The political arena is the
place where our laws are made which govern our society and which
affect the quality of human life. For this reason, the political arena

has become the moral arena, where good and evil collide in their battle for man's mind and heart. If Christians are absent from this locale, they not only abandon the field, but they forsake the people whose personal well-being depends upon the quality and equity of the law. Clyde Fant, professor at a seminary in the South, pointedly told his brethren, ". . . you cannot preach that you want a Christian America and not touch social [or world] issues." Pointing out that when his denomination was organized in the South in 1845, it adopted a statement upholding slavery, he concluded, ". . . to *defend* slavery is as much a *social* involvement as to *attack* it. The only difference is in conclusion." [8] When the church adopts an exilic style of ministry which disengages it from the life of the world, its very silence and inaction become the strongest kind of political decisions with far-reaching consequences!

We have been arguing that the heart of each man needs to be changed radically by an experience of God's grace and Christ's saving power, resulting in genuine conversion. But personal conversions must lead us to a deeper level in obedience to the Lordship of Christ, not only over the life of a church, but also over the life of the world. Individual conversions alone do not dismantle the institutional and social structures built by unconverted men and shared in often by professedly Christian men. These structures of prejudice, manned by massive engines of persuasion, selfishness and godlessness, continue to ride roughshod over the weak and voiceless. We can agree with those who say it would be better *if* there was enough love in every human heart to make open-housing laws unnecessary, or to make laws for fair-employment practices obsolete. But we must recognize the fallacy of assuming that individual and separate conversion experiences will automatically solve our common social problems! As matters stand, nearly any citizen, regardless of his social station or color or religion, is reasonably free to buy his own suit of clothes or his own make of car, depending upon personal preferences and the amount of money he has and wishes to spend. But no single person who lives in the city where the air is polluted can buy his share of clean air. It takes more than individual initiative or private action on the part of converted Christian people to tackle social problems like air or water pollution and to help change "the conditions of the road," which, as the young preacher saw, provide a dangerous habitat for man's life. Whenever law is not internalized in private conscience, as so often it turns out not to be, then conscience must be externalized in public law. Strangely enough, the man who says you can't legislate morals by act of Congress is not willing to dispense with stoplights, speed zones, and other traffic laws which define and limit our driving on streets and highways. If we cannot be content to let changed hearts change our traffic patterns, is it not self-apparent that we need corporate Christian action on the part of God's people in the church to relate its witness to the world of both personal and social needs of men throughout the whole wide earth? Most of us may have heard the story of a father's attempt to occupy his small son's energy, hoping for an uninterrupted evening of reading. He gave him what appeared to be a difficult jigsaw puzzle of the world cut up into many intricate pieces of the same shade and hue. In an astonishingly short time, the boy tugged at his father's sleeve because he had finished the puzzle. When asked how he had done it so quickly, the boy explained that on the other side there was a picture of a man. Because the colors and pieces fit together more easily, he worked on that side and, as he explained, "When I got the man right, I got the world right!" Unfortunately, jigsaw puzzles don't solve complex social problems on a global scale that easily! Nor do our separate conversions.

We do not well if in evangelism we neglect each man's need for the brokenness of his life to be made whole in Jesus Christ. Indeed, salvation, in its root meaning, includes that sense of wholeness. The meaning and the message of evangelism have been changed wherever the church has neglected the urgency of man's personal relationship to God. Evangelism requires our witness so that God may touch the human heart and men can become right with God in Jesus Christ. But the *other* side of that truth must be asserted quite as urgently. The task of evangelism is not completed by my single conversion, because the structures of society and the face of the world are not automatically changed by individual conversion. When we get the man right, the world is still not right. No single Christian has access to the world in such dimensions that it is automatically transformed as he is transformed. The structures of society have an autonomy and independence of their own, quite apart from our personal faith and our own existence as individuals.

An exodus from our exilic bondage in Babylon can free the church to fulfill the *full* dimensions of its evangelistic mission as we follow Christ from Bethlehem, serving as the continuing instrument of his incarnate ministry.

9
An Exodus from Haran to Antioch and Beyond

Chapter 1 traced the size and scope of the *Exodus from the Church* and set the stage for *An Exodus for the Church*. Weak and impotent, the church seems stalled by its bondage inwardly and outwardly. Church leadership, at all levels, feels trapped. Nothing less than a new exodus for the church can free the church to fulfill its Christian mission in evangelism.

In Chapter 2 we have claimed that the *Exodus from Egypt* and its bondage must lead us by way of Emmaus, because without the presence and power of a living Christ, the church has no good news to share in evangelistic witness and no power for its own continued existence.

In Chapter 3, we have described the needed *Exodus from Athens* and our captivity to our unexamined assumptions which continue to cripple the church both in understanding its message and in developing its evangelistic and missionary strategy. *An Exodus from Athens* can lead us from the unexamined life which frustrates our efforts to follow Christ in our own time.

In Chapter 4, we have examined our captivity in Nicea, which signifies our bondage to unreformed creeds which create meaning barriers in the church's efforts to communicate the gospel to its own century and to the "outside" world. *An Exodus from Nicea* is needed to free the church for witness.

In Chapter 5, we have called for *An Exodus from Jerusalem,* from our institutional intractability and idolatry which frustrate the capacity of the church to cope with change, both in its own life and in responding to the needs of its environment.

In Chapter 6, we offered our conviction that because of our captivity to culture and to social conventions, the church cannot effectively evangelize the world because we are asking men to come to a "national" Jesus. Only our *Exodus from Rome* will free the church to win men to the Christ above culture.

In Chapter 7, we have traced the manner in which the church has trapped itself by adopting the style of a special, rather than a universal, priesthood. This restricted ministry limits us as "a tribe of Levi" to take care of special things amid "religious" precincts and practices. *An Exodus from Sinai* can free the church to follow Jesus in his servant ministry in behalf of the world.

In Chapter 8, we have spoken to the theme that the church has likewise unwittingly embraced the exilic style of life which God's people experienced in their Babylonian captivity. This style of ministry is one of disengagement and historical absenteeism. We have affirmed that *An Exodus from Babylon to Bethlehem* can free the church to become the continuing body of Christ's incarnational style of ministry. This exodus will enable us to combine man's personal need for God's love and forgiveness with the need to take history, the structures of society, and the life of the nation as seriously as God had done so, as revealed in the Scriptures. Evangelism is nothing less than "bringing men to Jesus," one by one; but it also requires us to participate in God's purposes to renew the earth so his will may be done on earth even as it is done in heaven.

Last of all, in this chapter, we are calling for *An Exodus from Haran to Antioch and Beyond* (cf. Genesis 12:1-4). Haran is the Hebrew word for crossroads, where the church stands today in the midst of its bondage. God stands with us and says, "I have set before you a way of life and a way of death; choose life that you may live!" (See Deuteronomy 30:19.) An exodus from Haran must lead us "beyond Antioch." In the book of Acts Antioch was the launching center for thrusting the Christian witness into the life of the world and to the regions beyond! (Cf. Acts 13:1-3.)

An obscure text in Genesis (11:32) sets the stage for our discussion: "And Terah died in Haran." Terah was the father of Abraham and lived in Ur of the Chaldees. Evidently he had gathered his goods and his family to leave Ur and to journey into Canaan. One could infer that God's call had come to Terah before it came to Abraham; however, he got only as far as Haran, which in the Hebrew means "crossroads." There, on the crossroads of the main caravan routes between the East and the West, Terah settled down. He sought safety and security rather than risk and involvement. Perhaps this text stands as a sign for all of us who temporize with our difficulties, who compromise our highest ideals, and who mortgage our future so heavily that life has no other options but to foreclose. If it is true that men do have forever, it is also true that institutions do not have that long. The opportunities which pause on our doorstep as a church will not wait for us forever. There may be safety and shelter and security in Haran, but, as a people of God, our destiny is wrapped up in faithfulness to our mission with all of its uncertainty and its risks. Terah missed what he sought and he died in Haran. Abraham went out by faith and found what his father missed! The contemporary church faces the decision of Terah or Abraham. We are at the crossroads because God reveals himself to us, as to Moses, as "Jehovah"—not only "I am what I am," but "I will be what I will be" (cf. Exodus 3:13-14). In words akin to Ernest Bloch, the church can say of herself, "Man is he who is not yet." [1] To be open to the future of faith requires a

new exodus from Haran, from all the places where the church has
settled down into a life of escape rather than engagement, and of
truancy rather than trust.

But if we see the church humbled by her impotence and
weakness, ignored because of her stammering witness and her
cautious irrelevance, let us remember that God can turn weakness
into power. Israel was overpowered by the wealth, power, and
might of Egypt, Assyria, Babylon, Persia, Greece, and Rome. But,
as George Adam Smith tells us, it was the faith of this obscure
people, full of weakness, "which offered an explanation of history,
claimed the future," [2] and gained the assurance that the largest
forces of the world were working for its ends. If God's people,
today, are willing to link their lives to the final purposes of God,
they, too, out of weakness, can be made strong! God's agenda has
been filled with causes which men prematurely wrote off as "lost
and hopeless."

In the midst of prevailing despair and hopelessness, the thirty-
second chapter of Jeremiah provides us with an example of the
audacious faith which is required of us today. In the tenth year of
Zedekiah, king of Judah, or the eighteenth year of
Nebuchadnezzar, the city of Jerusalem was besieged by the
Babylonian army. Jeremiah, himself, was a prisoner in the
guardhouse of the royal palace because he had dared to prophesy
the doom of the city. The siege was so severe, over a period of some
eighteen months, that mothers were eating their own children
because of the ordeal of famine. In the midst of that hopeless and
discouraging situation, a kinsman of Jeremiah came to the prison
cell to ask him to exercise his right of inheritance to a piece of
property upon which the Babylonian army was seemingly at the
present moment encamped. Jeremiah, feeling that this represented
a dramatic opportunity to act in behalf of the fulfillment of the
divine purpose, responded affirmatively to his cousin's request. He
did not ask for a compromise purchase price, he did not ask for a
bargain; but he signed the deed, sealed it, secured the necessary
public witnesses, and paid down the money in full. He explained
this audacious act in the face of hopeless despair by asserting, "The
time will come when houses and fields and vineyards shall again be

bought in this land." (See Jeremiah 32:15.) In the face of an apparently lost and hopeless cause in the life of the nation, doomed to destruction and to captivity, Jeremiah's act affirmed a promise of hope and confidence that the land would come back. God would be gracious. God would renew his covenant with his people.

If the history of Israel testifies to the renewing power of God's steadfast purposes which are able to overcome weakness and to inspire an undiscouraged hope, the experience of the church is no less encouraging. Despite the entrenched strength of the Roman Empire, the first-century church spread the faith with unstoppable fervor and contagion. After working with the New Testament sources in connection with his biblical translation, J. B. Phillips derides those of us who talk about the difficulties of our times as though we must wait for better ones before the Christian faith can flourish or the life of the church can be renewed. He observes that, as a matter of record, the faith took root in a hostile soil and spread in an environment whose climate was not always favorable! If we are tempted to think of our Christian mission as a lost cause, we should remember what God has done with causes which men had labeled as lost!

The contemporary missionary movement in its early days looked like a lost cause when Adoniram Judson, after seven years of suffering and privation, had so little to show for his work in Burma. The movement which had been launched on the faith and vision of William Carey appeared to be a lost and hopeless cause for Judson, with only one convert to the Christian faith! It looked like a lost cause for the Christian faith when David Livingstone, one arm limp and useless, came to the end of his life with so little to show for his sacrifice in Africa. It looked like a lost cause when Robert Morrison died without ever having gained entrance to the main gate of China. It looked like a lost cause for religious liberty and freedom of conscience when Roger Williams was banished from the New England colony of Massachusetts. But, in each case, because of a justifiable confidence in the faithfulness of God's purposes, a few audacious souls have dared to believe that "houses and fields and vineyards would again be bought in the land," that *lost* causes could be reclaimed! "The light still shines in the darkness for the darkness is not able to put out the light" (cf. John 1:5). In such a confidence the church can overcome her enemies within and without and pledge her faith and fealty to the unfinished business on God's agenda in our contemporary age.

We must share the skepticism of Robert F. Horton who refused to accept as an article of faith "that God who was so near to patriarchs and prophets in Canaan that they could hear Him speak and receive directions from His lips, is after all these ages of growing light . . . less near to us, less tangible, less audible, less real to us." [3] It is significant that in the summary of apostolic teaching recorded in 1 Corinthians 15, the verbs "died," "was buried," and "appeared" are all in the aorist tense, signifying once for all action fulfilled in time past. But the verb "rose" is in the perfect tense, which signifies action begun in the past which continues up to the present moment. The church in her weakness can believe in an exodus because the ever living Christ is the surety of a never dying church! An exodus means literally "a way out." A contemporary existential novelist looked at the predicament of modern man, and he was led to the conclusion that for man and his world there is "no exit." But the Christian faith affirms, "I thank God, there is a way out, an exodus through Jesus Christ."

We have been asking for an exodus *for* the church, and that will require corporate church actions by congregations and other church bodies. But when the word of the Lord comes, it singles us out of the crowd so that we know we as individuals are being addressed and called by God. An exodus for the church will not let us elude our need for a personal exodus of our own, where we, too, like Terah, have settled down in Haran.

Some years ago, Dr. Karl Menninger wrote a book entitled *Man Against Himself*. From his long practice in the field of psychiatric medicine, Dr. Menninger had reached the conclusion that "Whoever studies the behavior of human beings . . . must reckon with an enemy within the lines." He notes the tendency within men which leads them to join forces in attacking their very own existence. Doctors and their allies in medicine must help patients to refrain "from doing things which favor the disease rather than the recovery." Bad as those malignancies are which may afflict people physically, Menninger sees as worse the malignant attitudes which lead people to "mismanage" their lives, while using their energies destructively upon themselves, their family, their jobs, their friends, as well as the institutions to which they belong. [4]

Most of us have had firsthand experiences which confirm Menninger's observations. There is "an enemy"—an Adversary—a Satan—a Devil—"within the lines." This malevolent presence within a man's life explains why man's best efforts go awry; why man acts irrationally; why man mismanages his life and spoils those relationships in the home, or on the job or in the church, which ought to be filled with the most meaning.

But this experience of evil is why the gospel comes as "good news." A Savior has come into the world! In sending his Son, Jesus Christ, God has acted to overcome the enemy. As Christians, we are assured that God's Spirit enters into our lives personally to give us power to prevail over the Adversary and to help us overcome a long history of frustrating failures and humiliating defeats. Because we know that God has received us and justified us, we do not have to use our energy to justify ourselves or to buy love and acceptance. We are set free to love others for the right reasons!

Has the enemy within your lines met his match in Jesus Christ? Until you accept his acceptance and live with his fortifying strength within you, you must continue to be "man against himself." Whatever you touch will be spoiled by selfishness, because until his sin is forgiven, a man insists on "mismanaging his life"! With Christ, Christians still face a determined foe; without Christ, no man can hope to overcome the Enemy! "If God be for us, who can be against us?" But if the final forces of the universe stand against us, who can be for us?

Paul Tournier speaks of the sense of personal commitment which should characterize our relationship to Christ and, at the same time, create an expectancy in our daily life and witness. "What I have to do," says Tournier, "is to put my signature at the foot of a blank page on which I will accept whatever God wishes to write. I cannot predict what he will put on this blank contract as my life proceeds—but I give my signature today." [5] One could add, not only are we unable to predict all the details of God's agenda either for the church or for ourselves, but we may also easily be mistaken in what we ascribe to his hand. But an exodus from Haran, the crossroads where God is waiting, surely that is his call to the church—and to you and to me!

Let me conclude with a Christmas letter from a mother who writes: "My son is in the army. He may never come back. He has a little girl and I am wondering if she and her generation will be different. Or must the same old cycle go on—hating, arming, killing?" Her words represent the petition of every mother and of every father who wants and who waits for the people of God in every church to lead them out of their bondage and captivity in a new exodus to life and hope.

Notes

Chapter 1

[1] *Yearbook of American Churches,* Edition for 1971 (New York: Council Press, 1971), p. 223.

[2] Louis Cassels, *The Evening Bulletin* (Philadelphia), March 14, 1970, p. 7.

[3] Kenneth W. Thompson, "The Perils of Polarization," *Christianity and Crisis,* vol. 30, no. 4 (Mar. 16, 1970), pp. 43-44.

[4] James E. Dittes, *The Church in the Way* (New York: Charles Scribner's Sons, 1967), p. 142.

[5] Harry Levinson, *The Exceptional Executive: A Psychological Conception* (Cambridge, Mass.: Harvard University Press, 1968), pp. 6-7; cf. 12-72.

[6] Cecil Northcott, "The Passing of the Parson," *The Christian Century,* vol. 85, no. 17 (April 24, 1968), pp. 509-510.

[7] Quoted by Jeffrey K. Hadden, "The Confession of 1967: A Case Study in Status Politics," *The Christian Ministry*, vol. 1, no. 2 (Jan., 1970), p. 25.

Chapter 2

[1] Anders Nygren, *The Gospel of God*, trans. L. J. Trinterud (Philadelphia: The Westminster Press, 1951), pp. 29-30.

[2] H. R. Mackintosh, *The Originality of the Christian Message* (New York: Charles Scribner's Sons, 1920), p. 26.

[3] C. H. Dodd, *The Authority of the Bible* (London: Nisbet & Co., Ltd., 1948), p. 231

[4] John 21:25 seems like an exaggerated hyperbole if the writer is thinking only of Jesus' public ministry. But I wonder if he may not be linking his thought to the beginning of his book, John 1:1-4, and the preincarnate work of the Living Word?

Chapter 3

[1] Herbert Butterfield, *Christianity and History* (New York: Charles Scribner's Sons, 1950), p. 89.

[2] Arthur Koestler, *The Ghost in the Machine* (New York: The Macmillan Company, 1967), pp. 261-262.

[3] *Ibid.*

[4] Karl Menninger, *The Vital Balance* (New York: The Viking Press, Inc., 1963), pp. 389-390.

[5] William Temple et al, *Towards the Conversion of England* (Westminster, England: The Press and Publications Board of the Church Assembly, 1945), p.10.

[6] *Ibid.*, p. 133.

Chapter 4

[1] Edwin Hatch, *The Influence of Greek Ideas on Christianity* (New York: Harper & Row, Publishers, 1957), p. 1.

[2] Quoted in *Judson Journal*, vol. 30, no. 1 (Spring, 1966), pp. 3, 4, 30. Published by American Baptist Board of Education and Publication, Valley Forge, Pa.

[3] Samuel H. Miller, Address given at Crozer Theological Seminary, Chester, Pa.

[4] J. V. Langmead Casserley, *Apologetics and Evangelism* (Philadelphia: The Westminster Press, 1962), p. 95. Copyright © MCMLXII, W. L. Jenkins. Used by permission.

[5] *Ibid.*, p. 97.

[6] L. P. Jacks, *Religious Perplexities* (New York: George H. Doran Company, 1923), p. 38.

[7] John Oman, *Vision and Authority* (London: Hodder and Stoughton, Revised edition, 1929), p. 52.

[8] Dale R. Turner, Unpublished address to annual meeting of the Kansas Baptist Convention, Ottawa, Kansas.

[9] Edwin Lewis, *The Faith We Declare* (Nashville: Abingdon Press, 1939), pp. 93-94.

[10] D. M. Baillie, *God Was in Christ* (New York: Charles Scribner's Sons, 1948), p. 109.

[11] George Orwell, *Nineteen Eighty-four* (New York: Harcourt Brace Jovanovich, Inc., 1949), pp. 51-54. Reprinted by permission of Brandt & Brandt.

Chapter 5

[1] Harvey Cox, *The Secular City*, Revised Edition (New York: The Macmillan Company, 1965), p. 202. Copyright © Harvey Cox, 1965, 1966. Published in England by S. C. M. Press Ltd.

[2] *Ibid.*

[3] Quoted by Lawrence K. Frank, "The Need for a New Political Theory," *Daedalus*, vol. 96, no. 3 (Summer, 1967), p. 816.

[4] Carlyle Marney, Address given to the American Baptist Convention, June 4, 1960, Rochester, N.Y.

[5] James Baldwin, *Go Tell It on the Mountain* (New York: The Dial Press, 1963), pp. 39-40.

[6] Marvin Bower, *The Will to Manage* (New York: McGraw-Hill Book Company, 1966), pp. 81-82. Used with permission of McGraw-Hill Book Company.

[7] *Ibid.*

Chapter 6

[1] Walt Kelly, "Pogo Looks at the Abominable Snowman," *The Saturday Review*, August 30, 1958, pp. 7ff.

[2] L. L. L. Golden, *Only By Public Consent* (New York: Hawthorn Books, Inc., 1968), p. 4. By permission of Hawthorn Books, Inc.

[3] George Orwell, *Nineteen Eighty-Four* (New York: Harcourt Brace Jovanovich, Inc., 1949), p. 285. Reprinted by permission of Brandt & Brandt.

[4] W. E. Orchard, *The Outlook for Religion* (New York: Cassell and Company, Ltd., 1917), p. 100.

[5] *Ibid.*, p. 147.

[6] W. H. Auden, "The Unknown Citizen," *The Collected Poetry of W. H. Auden* (New York: Random House, 1967), p. 141.

[7] Eric Russell Bentley, *The Playright as Thinker* (New York: Meridian Books, 1955), Foreword, p.xv.

[8] Martin Luther King, Jr., Unpublished address to the annual meeting of the American Baptist Convention, May 24, 1962.

⁹ J. V. Langmead Casserley, *The Bent World* (New York: Oxford University Press, Inc., 1955), p. 123.

¹⁰ George Bernard Shaw, *Saint Joan of Arc*, Scene 5.

¹¹ W. A. Visser 'T Hooft, *The Renewal of the Church* (Philadelphia: The Westminster Press, 1956), pp. 69-72.

Chapter 7

¹ Mrs. James Ekstrand in *The Secret Place*, vol. 34, no. 4 (Jan. 10, 1972), p. 34.

² Advisory Commission of World Council of Churches, *The Christian Hope and the Task of the Church* (New York: Harper & Row, Publishers, 1954), pp. 18-19.

³ George Adam Smith, *The Book of Isaiah* (New York: A. C. Armstrong and Son, 1898), vol. 1, pp. 59-60.

⁴ Reuel L. Howe, *The Miracle of Dialogue* (New York: The Seabury Press, Inc., 1963). See especially Chapter 5, "The Participants in Dialogue."

⁵ Roger L. Cox, "Dostoevsky's Grand Inquisitor," *Cross Currents*, vol. 17, no. 4 (Fall, 1967), p. 443.

Chapter 8

¹ Readers who want a fuller treatment of this theme are directed to three articles:

(a) Robert N. Bellah, "Civil Religion in America," *Daedalus—Journal of the American Academy of Arts and Sciences* (Winter, 1967), pp. 1-21.

(b) Richard J. Neuhaus, "The War, the Churches, and Civil Religion," *The Annals of the American Academy of Political and Social Science* (Jan., 1970), pp. 128-140.

(c) LeRoy Moore, Jr., "From Profane to Sacred America: Religion and the Cultural Revolution in the United States," *Journal of the American Academy of Religion*, vol. 39, no. 3 (Sept., 1971), pp. 321-338.

² A. R. Vidler, *Christian Belief and This World*, as quoted in Douglas Webster, *What Is Evangelism?* (London: The Highway Press, 1964), p. 93.

³ John Oman, *Grace and Personality* (New York: The Macmillan Company, 1925), p. 81.

⁴ C. H. Dodd, *The Authority of the Bible* (London: Nisbet & Co., Ltd., 1948), p. 258.

⁵ C. S. Lewis, *Christian Behaviour* (New York: The Macmillan Company, 1944), pp. 13-14. See *Mere Christianity*, Copyright 1943, 1945, 1952 by The Macmillan Company. Published in England by Collins Publishers.

⁶ *Ibid.*, p. 15.

⁷ Karl Barth, *Community, State, and Church* (Garden City, N.Y.: Doubleday & Company, Inc., Anchor Books, 1960), pp. 184-185.

⁸ Clyde Fant, quoted in *The Kansas Baptist*, November, 1968, p. 3.

Chapter 9

¹ Ernest Bloch, "Man as Possibility," *Cross Currents,* vol. 18, no. 3 (Summer, 1968), pp. 273-283.

² George Adam Smith, *The Book of Isaiah* (New York: A. C. Armstrong and Son, 1898), vol. 2, p. 151.

³ Robert F. Horton, *Verbum Dei: Yale Lectures on Preaching, 1893* (New York: The Macmillan Company, 1893), p. 66.

⁴ Karl Menninger, *Man Against Himself* (New York: Harcourt Brace Jovanovich, Inc., 1938), pp. 4-9.

⁵ Paul Tournier, *The Adventure of Living* (New York: Harper & Row, Publishers, 1965), p. 195.